RESEARCH AND REFERENCE SOURCES IN MANAGEMENT AND BUSINESS

RESEARCH AND REFERENCE SOURCES IN MANAGEMENT AND BUSINESS

Compiled By :
Jayendra F. Pandya
Deputy Liibrarian

Introduction By :
Prof. Abhinandan K. Jain
Prof. in Marketing

Forword By :
Ashok Jambhekar
Librarian

VIKRAM SARABHAI LIBRARY

BOOKWELL PUBLICATIONS

Published By :
BOOKWELL PUBLICATIONS
24/4800, Ansari Road, Darya Ganj,
New Delhi-110002

ISBN : 81-85040-07-9

Price : Rs. 200.00

1st Edition : August, 1994

Pandya, Jayendra F.

Research and Reference Sources in Management and Business, Delhi. Bookwell. 1994

1. Management-Reference sources 2. Business-Reference sources 3. Management-Research sources 4. Business-Research sources I. Title

Printed By :
New Era Printers
161-A, Dhaka Village,
Delhi-110009

CONTENTS

INTRODUCTION

Obtaining right information in right time from a information storehouse (i.e. library) is extremely difficult for a student who either does not know what is available or does not understand how to find it. I was confronted during my student days at the institute, with such situations when I spent a lot of time and yet was not able to get the information I was looking for. One of the factors for such a situation was the lack of knowledge about the collection and the information content of the collection. The difficulties compound when one is looking for primary sources of information or references on specific concepts or subjects. A volume on Research and Reference Sources in Management and Business by Mr. Jayendra F. Pandya, Dy. Librarian of Vikram Sarabhai Library at IIM Ahmedabad comes as an invaluable help to researchers and academics in management.

The volume describes catalogues of books and directories of journals on management which could be used for selection of books/journals by institutions. Chapters on subject bibliographies, current awareness services, indexing services, and abstracting services would be of great help in identifying appropriate pieces of literature for researching particular topics. Chapters on reference sources on on going research (on dectoral dissertations and working papers etc.) and statistical data (including census) would help the researcher in identifying most recent conceptual as well as contextual material. Annotated listing of important journals categorised by major management and related subjects is of immense help in readily locating relevant journal (s).

Chapter on On-Line Databases provides a glimpse of fast changing character of the nature of help available to researchers for locating literature. It also underlies a need for researchers to be familiar with such sources and/or a need for specialised agencies to help researchers in locating appropriate literature.

Appendices contain Bibliography on Research Mothodology, and Style Manuals and Thesis Writing which enhances the book's value as a reference tool /source itself. Exhibits at the end of this publication brings out the important process of searching for literature pictorially very well.

The volume could have further enhanced its value if it contained separate chapter on management cases and indicated locations where (in India) the spacific items are available. In any case, I think about 60 to 70 per cent of the items may be available in VSL, IIM Ahmedabad, and the libraries of all the four IIMs together cover almost all.

It is a commendable effort by Mr. J. F. Pandya. The volume would be of tremendous use to doctoral students, researchers, and teachers of management in locating right information in the least possible time

Prof. Abhinandan K. Jain

Prof. in Marketing

FOREWORD

In 1981, Mr. J.F. Pandya with Mr. M.C. Shah and Mr. G.J. Trivedi prepared a book describing the information sources in the disciplines of business and industry. The effort of theirs was widely appreciated for its information value and coverage. This book is a companion volume to the above as it extends coverage to the disciplines of social sciences and management.

In the present age of information explosion and the consequent growth and spread of literature, the task of researcher of locating the sources of the precise information required by him has became extremely difficult. Scatter of relevant information being large, due to rapidly increasing specialization in research, further complicates his work of location of relevant information. The library staff has, therefore, a greater and vital role in establishing contact between the right reader at the right time, although it is not easy one. In the context of the library profession, this is termed as reference service. It is an integral part of the library services. Through the assistance rendered, the researcher is not only provided the information, but also acquainted with catalogues, bibliographical tools such as indexing and abstracting periodicals, subject bibliographies etc, statistical information, specialized journals, handbooks, data bases, and various other reference tools.

Mr. Pandya has done a great job by bringing together the sources of information which provide current as well as retrospective information.

The sources as classified by him are :

- Current Research in the field
- State of art reviews
- Latest books and current articles from Journals
- Government publications including official statistics
- Trend Reports
- Conference papers

- Theses, dissertations, and Research in progress
- Data Banks
- Working papers and discussion papers
- Documents on Research Methodology
- Documents on style manuals and thesis writing.

The book is a valuable guide for the location of the relevant literature i.e. the literature search, which every researcher/ scholar has to do. The reference value has enhanced by the inclusion of both macro-documents and micro-documents.

I am confident that this book prepared by Mr. Pandya under the Seed Money Project scheme will have appeal to a wide audience like Librarians, Library Schools, besides the Researchers for whom it is mainly targeted.

July, 1994

Ashok Jambhekar

PREFACE

The various intellectual activities are involved inpreparing a written text, whether it be an article, a technical report, a paper for conference/seminar, a project report, a research report and thesis or a academic/research dissertation. It is the purpose of this publication to acquaint the teachers, researchers, and FPM students of management and business with the available reference/ research sources and facilitate location of the needed information for their research study. Researchers have to depend on the library to a great extent. They will save their valuable time if they know how to refer the library effectively, and familiarise themselves with the scope, nature of information and contents of various types of reference/research sources available in the library. This publication attempts to describe published research sources in management and business. Both the Indian and foreign publications are included with annotations wherever possible. Published and semi-published information is important to the extent that it enables them to build upon the work and experience of others. More than 20 research sources with examples are listed in detail and their importance and use explained. Bibliography of books on "Research Methology" and" Theses Writing" are as essential and important for any research activity as the reference sources. Therefore, without them, the publication would have remained incomplete, and hence these are listed towards the end of the volume.

I welcome suggestions and comments for further improvements of this work.

Vikram Sarabhai Library **J.F. Pandya**
IIM, Ahmedabad **Deputy Librarian**

ACKNOWLEDGEMENT

I would like to express my gratitude to Prof. Anil K. Gupta, the then Chairman, Research Committee for sanctioning the funds for carrying out this 'Project'.

Prof. A. K. Jain Professor in Marketing at the Institute has been a great source of inspiration in compilation of this publication. Guidance and the support provided throughout the presentation of this publication has been extremely useful. I express my gratitude to him.

Perhaps, the most important critic of this work has been Mr. Ashok Jambhekar, Librarian, IIM-A as his valuable comments are always useful and enabled me to sharpen my thinking in many areas. My deep sense of gratitude to him.

Hima B. Soni assisted me in library search and preparing entries for the reference sources and bibliographies - thanks to her.

I would also like to express my appreciation to Muralidharan K.N. who typed the manuscript with skill and great patience.

Deep gratitude is due to my wife Aruna, who not only constantly encouraged me, but also enabled me to devote all my spare time to such works, I had undertaken.

Thanks are also due to Mr. Manmohan Singh Khurana of M/s. BOOKWELL, Delhi for the timely publication of this work.

DEDICATED TO

IIM'S

FPM STUDENTS

FOR WHOM I WORK

AND

FROM WHOM I LEARN

REFERENCE WORKS AND THE RESEARCH

Management education has emerged in the last three decades as one of the distinctive feature in the Indian University Systems. There are today nearly 60 university departments, 4 IIMs' and about 35 other instituions which offer variety of management educational programmes. Besides the management schools and institutions, sectoral management institutions have also been established. The programmes conducted in these various types of institutions are helping to fulfil the objectives of promoting linkages between the management, educational institutions and industry, business and government. All these institutions have fairly good modern library with a few exception. Library is regarded as a service to assist the faculty, research community, Ph.D. and Post Graduate Students and the participants of various short term program to make the effective use of its resources and services for their research, knowledge, and skill development.

Libraries in the educational and research institutions are described as laboratories. Late Dr. Vikram Sarabhai, the founder Director of IIM-A had once said that "the library is the soul of the institutions and no institution can ever develop its academic and research activities without a well equipped and scientifically organized library and its services". Now-a-days, the libraries/information centres have become the centres of real laboratories and tools for study, teaching and research. Libraries play a vital role more so in research and academic institutions. The volume of information being generated now-a-days has created an enormous problem of control. There are various types of library and information services and a vast amount of information sources available to meet the requirements of the research community. The information storage and the retrieval system should be so designed to meet the academic and research needs of the institute/organization. The transfer of information is of the utmost importance to research and development. The research worker should know how to tap libraries or sources of information and should have right attitudes to the task of finding relevant information and to approach it with confidence, and in doubt he should develop an attitude of open minded questioning; and approach it in the spirit of finding out about its resources and how best to use them. Every research library has a variety of reference books or tools which were meant for quick and easy consultation. A researcher will save a great deal of labour and time if he is familiar with various types of reference tools and made use of them whenever need arises during his research work. A researcher may spend hours or weeks to locate a piece of information in books or journals which may be readily available in one of these tools.

There are vairous types of reference tools, but the library user should know and understand how to use these resources effectively like the catalogue; bibliographies, periodical indexes and abstracting journals; statistical publications; reference works such as encyclopaedias; yearbooks and directories, data bases on- line and off-line both. Your success in using efficiently the material available in your library, will determine to a great extent your production of research paper, research project or dissertation.

At the nucleus of an organized research programmes are developed, the library should cover all appropriate fields in sufficient depth and scope to provide an accurate picture of the historical developments in the field as well as pertinent and up-to-date data.

Today is an age of information technology. Information is power is an old dictum yet it is vital to stay ahead in today's world. Right information at right time is what management information system is all about.

There is an information explosion in business and management. Now a days, the information has become the fifth basic need after air, water, food and shelter. Information production is increasing rapidly due to activities and more and more educational facilities. The literature on management, business, industry and its related fields has been accumulating for the years at an accelerated pace. The complexity of business activities demand the awareness of the latest management techniques.

No progress in any field would be possible without research. All governments around the globe spend huge amount of resources to carry out research through its various agencies, departments, universities, institutions etc., in almost all fields like, agriculture, business and industry, science, communication, transportation, housing, medicine, energy, aeronautics, new products, education, engineering, technology and various other fields.

Also, with more and more unviersities and institutions taking up management research, training and teaching, more and more teachers and researchers are getting involved in the publication of project reports, research findings, surveys, thesis and dissertations. It is roughly estimated that about 1700 teachers and equal number of research workers are engaged either in teaching and research and more than 20,000 students are studying in the different Universities Department of Business Management, and other Management Institutes. The government, universities, institutions, unions, trade and professional associations and business organizations put out massive amount of primary and secondary data.

A large volume of writing has been done by teachers and research workers in the business schools. Information production is increasing rapidly from time to time due to increased number of publication, research activities, educational facilities etc. Rapid growth of information has resulted in increased literature production. Literature production is so enormous that it has been assessed that 20 to 30 million titles are published every year. Influence of information explosion on individuals and societies has resulted in establishment of organized information centres.

The use of databases, abstracting, indexing services and resource sharing have become part of essential activities of every library. Information is very valuable and the value can be assessed only when it is applied or used. The information must be acquired from different sources and has to be made available to the users. To promote access to the information required by the users, the library and documentation centres are established.

The rising tide of publications had brought in turn its demand and adequate means provided to evaluate; organize and direct towards its maximum use. When the availability of information is stupendous, one is bound to have a feeling of 'lost' in it unless he familiarises himself with the sources of information in his/her field of interest.

The business libraries can play a vital role and also can be most helpful if the techniques of using its many sources are known. Acquaintance with the variety of sources offered by such libraries can be of immense value to business research. In every research study undertaken, the researcher is seeking information on his topic. He has to tap all the relevant and available resources.

Research can be described as :

Research is an interactual process where a problem is perceived, divided into constituent elements, and analyzed in the light of certain basic assumptions, valid and relevant data are collected, hypotheses (if any) are rejected, amended or provided by objective testing (Shera, 1965)

–a systematic inquiry to discover facts, to find new truths, to avoid the status quo (or)

–an orderly, exhaustive investigation to test accepted principles of conclusions (or)

–a diligent objective examination to find new truths and revise accepted principles or conclusions.

The first step in carrying out the inquiry is to find out whether someone has already dealt with the subject in past i.e. in an article or in a book, or someone has been working exactly on same topic/subject. Under such circumstances, there is always a danger of duplication or near duplication of the same work in different places. To avoid duplication or near- duplication of the same work in different places, there are various forms of reference sources which give information on researches conducted, in progress, and completed in different educational institutions. Any researcher's first question is: "what kind of materials/aids are available and from where".

One of the main problem faced by students/scholars engaged in research is in locating the documentary sources. Many students are not able to review the literature systematically in his/her field of research because of lack of awareness of literature. A proper methodical approach to data collection will help the researcher in organizing the research project/thesis/dissertation.

A chart showing some of the methodical steps for any research/project writing is given here which may be helpful to the fresh researcher.

The researcher seeking data for research has several avenues open to him. Some part of data required for research is already available in books, journals, government publications, institutional publications, corporate, association and societies publications, conference proceedings, working papers and other reference sources and services like bibliographies, indexing, abstracts, and current awareness services, in print and other forms of media like microforms, sound cassette, films, videos or tapes slides etc. An attempt is made to describe the scope of printed data and offer some help in finding the specific kind of information desired. The following pages describe selected useful reference sources and services, in business and management and related disciplines from which helpful information for conducting research can be obtained. The reference sources described are classified under the following headings.

Books

Journals

Financial/Economic Papers

Cumulative Indexes

Bibliographies

Indexing Services

Abstracting Services

Research Sources:
- Research Completed
- Research in Progress

Research Reports/Monographs

Academic Periodicals
Statistical Publications
Census Publications 1981, 1991
Current Awareness Services
Selective Dissemination of Information
Working Papers
Reviews
Chambers of Commerce and Industry
Corporation Publications
Trade Associations
Conference/Seminar Proceedings
On-Line Databases/Systems

BOOKS

LIBRARY CATALOGUE:

The most important and convenient source of reference for the books in any research library is the library catalogue which is an important and a convenient tool. Library collection are indexed alphabetically in the card catalogue; each work is catalogued under author's last name, title and subject. Each work is also classified with call numbers so that it can be located easily and quickly. Each card contains the full bibliographical details about each book which allows the reader to decide the books of the interest. The libraries classify their publications in order to bring together those on a particular subject. In short, a catalogue is a bibliography of one library's collection of books and other printed material. Whenever an inquiry about a particular book/subject is made, and it is ascertained that a book has been published on the subject, the first step is to examine the catalogue of a library. Since, it is very difficult for a library to obtain all books, the information about a particular book which one require may not be available. To locate information about the books not available in a library, the bibliography of published books is an important source. Important bibliographies are described below:

The Basic Business Library: Core Resources. ed. by B.S. Schlessinger. / Phoonix, Oryx Press, 1983.

The publication is divided in three parts, core list of printed reference sources; literature of business reference and business libraries 1976-1982; and business reference sources and services - Essays.

Books in Print, 1989-90. 8v. New York, R.R. Bowker, 1989.

The 42nd edition of BIP is in eight volumes. It lists approximately 8,00,000 titles available from 30,000 United States Publishers. Volume 1, 2 and 3 are on alphabetically arranged author index; volume 4, 5 and 6 are an alphabetically arranged title index. Vol. 7 contains books out of print and out of stock. Vol. 8 contains information about all the publishers whose titles are listed in the first sever volumes. Eight indexes are included.

British National bibliography. British Library bibliographic Services. vol.1: Subject Catalogue. Vol. 2 : Indexes.

The objects of the BNB are to list new works published in the British Isles to describe each work in detail into give the subject matter of each work as precisely as possible. The bibliography is in three sections. 1. Classified subject catalogue; 2. arranged alphabetically by authors, titles, editors, series etc. and the subject index. It gives exhaustive index to the subject matter of books.

Business and Economics Books and Serials in Print. New York, R.R. Bowker Company.

It is very comprehensive computer-produced lists of books on business, financial and economic literature. It is very useful for the business libraries. It has subject, author and title indexes.

Cumulative Book Index. (Monthly except August) N.Y., H.W. Wilson Co.)

The index is comprehensive and a permanent record of accurate, complete and timely information on English language books published each year around the world.

INDIAN BOOKS IN PRINT - 1991; a Bibliogrpahy of Indian Books Published in English language, ed. by Sher Singh. 3v. Delhi, Indian bibliographies Bureau, 1988.

IBP, 1991 containing nearly 3,00,000 entries reporting about 1,00,000 titles. Vol. I - Authors; Vol. 2 - Titles; and Vol. 3 Subject guide. The subject guide contains a detailed information about books published in the country, and it classified according to the Dewey Decimal Classification with feature headings and the Directory of Indian Publishers with complete addresses.

Indian National Bibliography, Calcutta, Central Reference Library, (1958-)

The Indian National Biboiogrpahy is a classified record of current Indian publications in fourteen major Indian languages including English received under the delivery of books Act, in the National Library, Calcutta.

In 1958 this National Bibliography made its appearance as a quarterly with annual cumulations till 1963. The periodicity was changed to monthly from January 1964, with annual cumulations.

This Bibliography is in three parts, classified under author and title and subject index respectively.

Library of Congress Catalogue-Books: Subjects: A cumulative list of works represented by Library of Congress Printed Cards, 1950-

Books-subjects is designed to serve as a continuing and cumulative subject bibliography of record works currently received and catalogued by LC and other American libraries. It constitutes a reference and research tool providing a basic subject control over a large portion of the world's current output of significant books.

Subject Guide to books in Print 1957-. 2v. New York, R.R. Bowker Co.

It lists all the books new and old in various subject categories with full ordering information.

JOURNALS

Information in journals is inveriably upto date than information in books. Journals are published regularly and as such they are more efficient in dissemination of current information. They disseminate the results of research and serve as a forum for analytical discussions; new ideas; theories; processes and techniques and nascent thoughts on a subject are published in journals within weeks of their formulation while it may take more time before they appear in book form. Even some of the information appearing in journals is not published at all in books. A considerable amount of recent information required for research in management and business can be found in journals. Broadly, the journals may be grouped as (a) Academic Journals (b) Professional and Technical Journals (c) Business and Trade Journals and (d) Financial Dailies. Academic journals are published by business management schools, universities, research institutions, learned societies, etc. which are primarily used for research work, advanced study in subject. Some learned periodicals are totally devoted to the research in specific area. Periodicals are also published by government, professional and trade associations and organizations, banks and by private bodies which cover a wide range of topics. They also provide the useful information, besides articles of interest and statistics to teachers and researchers.

The following directories are useful for the selection of periodicals:

Directory of Periodicals Published in India. 2d ed. Comp. by S. Kaur and P. Sapra. New Delhi, Sapra and Sapra Pub.

The present edition enlists about 7,200 titles including 160 title cross references, 110 subject cross references, and 178 dis-continued and ceased titles. These are arranged under 118 subject headings and 125 subheadings. The Directory is arranged in 3 section. Section 1 contains bibliographic information for periodicals classified by subject. Section 2, has status unknown/unconfirmed titles and the Section 3 contains title index.

Standard Periodical Directory. New York: Oxbridge Communications, Annual, 1963-

This directory contains information on over 65,000 periodicals published in the United States and Canada. It is arranged by subject, and each entry includes title, publishing company, address, telephone, key staff names, description of contents, book review acceptance, year established, frequency and circulation, advertising and subscription rates, printing method, size, and color if used. There is also an index by title.

Ulrich's International Periodical Directory - 1989-90, 3v. 28thed. rev. New York. R.R. Bowker, 1989

The 28th edition of Ulrich's International Periodicals Directory continues its tradition of excellence in serials information. In addition to the many enhancements and changes introduced in the 27th edition, more new features have been added to assist users in the research and acquisitions of serials.

The 28th edition of Ulrich's contains information on more than 111,950 serials published throughout the world, arranged under 557 subject headings. More than 66,000 entries from the 27th edition have been updated to reflect the most current information available and more than 6,000 serials have been added. Vol. I of the Directory have the subject "Economics and Business" from pages 553 to pages 942 i.e. about 390 pages listing about 12,000 periodicals on Economics, Industry, Management and its related subjects.

FINANCIAL/ECONOMIC PAPERS

A busy executive, either in business, trade or industry, financial institutons or in government should be aware of what is going on in his work of interest in the country as well as in the world. Financial papers are essential daily reading for the business community. They are the voluminous source of latest information about the financial, industrial and companies news. They also publish articles on management techniques.

The information about the companies published in the form of news items includes abstracts of annual reports, details about company meetings, annual speeches of Chairman/Managing Directors, news about appointments and resignations, award of contracts, labour disputes, stock-exchange prices, sales promotion, establishment of new companies, organizational mergers, government notifications, policies etc. etc. The following Indian and Foreign dailies are useful.

Economic Times: Ahmedabad, Bangalore, Bombay, Calcutta, Delhi.

Financial Express. Bombay, Delhi, Madras, Bangalore

Business Standard. Calcutta

The Observer of Business and Politics. Bombay, New Delhi

Asian Wall Street Journal. Hong Kong

Financial Times. London

New York Times. New York

Wall Street Journal. New York

Special Supplements:

Often, financial dailies publish special supplements on industries, and products, conferences and seminars and also on its various aspects. The articles in such supplements are written by the specialists in the subject or by the prominent leaders/ professionals of the industry are very much informative and useful. They analyse the survey reports which are very useful to academics, research and business community.

Indexes to Financial Dailies

Unfortunately, no financial newspapers in India publishes indexes eventhough they are very useful to researchers for retrospective search. In Ahmedabad edition of Economic Times, monthly index to articles appeared in the edit page during April 1992 has been published in the issue of 5th May 1992. This can be expanded in other areas also.

The following foreign papers published indexes:

1. Monthly Index to Financial Times. (Monthly with annual cumulation, 1982-)

2. New York Times Index. (Semi-Monthly with annual cumulation)

3. Wall Street Journal Index (Monthly with annual cumulation).

CUMULATIVE INDEXES

Almost all academic journals are compiling the annual index after the volume is complete. The index is published either in the last issue of the journals or in the first issue of the next volume. Sometimes, the annual index is published separately. In the same way, many of the national and interational academic journals are also publishing the cumulative indexes - may be for 10, 20, 40 or more years. Some journals have the policy of publishing the cumulative index in the journals itself and not separately as an independant publication. This is very important, quick and formidable source of scanning the literature on one's own research topic. The articles listed in cumulative indexes are mostly classified under the subjects and having the other indexes like author, title. It helps the researcher to know about all the articles of his interest for the last many years' under one cover, otherwise one has to go through all the pages or the annual indexes for all the years.

Every researcher have certain number of journals which are referred frequently. If the cumulative indexes of such journals, are located, it saves lot of his labour and time in searching the required literature. Some of the few published cumulative indexes are listed as examples.

Business History (1958-) (Q). London, Frank Cass. Business History, 1958-1990. A cumulative Index

The cumulative index lists all the contributions published in Business History since its inception in 1958.

Indian Journal of Agricultural Sciences: (A cumulative index of Vol. 1-54; 1983-1984, 1986. Jodhpur, Deepak Publishers

The journals started in 1931 transmitting the results of agricultural research to the researchers engaged in the field of Agriculture, Soil Science, Forestry, Horticulture, Floriculture etc.

Journal of Advertising (Q). U.S.A. Americal Academy of Advertising

Twenty-year index having 'Author Index' and 'Subject Index'. Published in Vol. 20, No. 4; December 1991.

Journal of Financial Economics. Vols. 1-30; 1974-1991.

Have subject and author index. Published in the issue of JFE, V. 30; No. 2; December 1991.

Journals of Public Economics. Vols. 1-40, 1990. Amsterdam, North-Holland. (Master Index)

Arrangement by authors only

Labour and Society. Vol. 1 (1976) - Vol. 14 (1989). Geneva, International Institute of Labour Studies, 1990.

Cumulative title, author and subject indexes.

Mathematical Programming. Master Index. Amsterdam, North Holland, 1990.

Sr. A: Vols. 34-41, 43-44

Sr/ B: Vols. 42 and 45

Study: Vols. 26-31

R & D Management. Oxford, Basil Blackwell

Vol. 21, No. 1; January 1991 issue contains the cumulative index from Vol. 11 to 20 (1981 to 1990)

SRA Journals Society of Research Administration. Chicago

Vol. 23, No. 1; Summer 1991 Subject index Vol. 1, through 22.

Vikalpa: The Journal for Decision Makers: Index to Vol. 1-12; 1976-1987. Ahmedabad, IIM, 1988.

Having subject index; author index, title index and list of subjects.

Administrative Science Quarterly and Harward Business Review publish cumulative indexes.

BIBLIOGRAPHIES

Bibliographies may be general, national or specific, some are comprehensive and selective having the important references on a particular subject.

Bibliographies are very useful in finding material on a specific subject or field. They include published material - books, chapters from books, reports, government documents, institutional publications, international agencies and government publications, periodical articles, irrespective of the fact whether they are available in a particular library or not. The bibliogrpahy is more useful if it is annotated. The bibliography dealing with a specific subject is going to be the most useful source of literature searching. Every business library should have a good selected collection of subject bibliographies suited to the needs of the users.

There are bibliographies appended to articles in periodicals, may be listed as "further readings" in books and after the chapter ends or separately at the end of the books. References are also given in the form of "footnotes" to books.

The bibliography may be considered as an extension to the catalogue for finding information and identifying publications, and should be available to the library users i.e. faculty, research workers, doctoral students and library professionals. For more specialized bibliographies related to the functional aspects of business and management one must firstly turn to library catalogues and bibliographies of bibliographies. The other sources can be the publication lists of relevant schools of management such as IIM's, AIMA, ASCI, MDI, XLRI, IRMA, and other University Departments of Business Management, and Institutions. They will provide a good insight into the range of the subject as they often compile bibliographies, short guides and reading lists on a variety of topics and can be obtained on request.

This is the preliminary investigation stage in research to know the literature available on the subjects.

Bibliographies on all subjects are listed in the following bibliography of bibliographies.

A Bibliography of Bibliographies on India. Kalia, D.R. & Jain, M.K. Delhi. Concept Publishing Co., 1975.

The book contains a total number of 1243 titles comprising bibliographies, library catalogues, documentation lists, abstracts, dissertation lists, serial catalogues etc. Most of the titles included are in English, but quite a good collection of material in Indian languages has been made available. Entries have been arranged by subject giving bibliographical details about each title. The arrangement of entries within the subject is alphabetical. Wherever necessary the entries have been annotated.

A Bibliography of Indian Bibliographies 1961-1980. Compiled and edited by K.K. Cochukoshy. Calcutta. Central Reference Library, 1985.

This bibliography is mainly based on the entries recorded in Indian National Bibliography between 1961-1980. The bibliography contains 655 entries according to broad subject headings, and having an Author-Title Index. A comprehensive subject index to the titles listed is given at the end.

Bibliographic Index; Cumulative Bibliography of Bibliographies. New York, Wilson, 1938- 3 times a year (April, August, December with annual cumulation).

The starting point for successful research for more than 50 years, this index is a subject index to bibliographies from social sciences to science and technology. This covers bibliographies published in books, pamphlets from more than 2800 periodicals regularly monitored. It lists bibliographies with 50 or more citations. Each entry provides complete information on the bibliography indexed and notes whether it is annotated.

A World Bibliography of Bibliographies and of Bibliographical Catalogues, Calenders, Abstracts, Digests, Indexes and the Like, by Theodore

Besterman, 5v. Geneva, Societus bibliographica, 1965-67.

This work is considered as a classic. This records well over 1,17,000 fully collected volumes of bibliography in over 50 languages. It is international in scope, covers books, manuscripts and patent abridgements in all subjects, with a time range from 15th century to 1963. The entries have been arranged alphabetically under 15000 heading and subheadings. Vol. 5 is devoted to Index, which provides names of authors, editors, translators, titles of periodicals, names of libraries and archieves. It records about 80,000 bibliographies arranged by subject.

SOME EXAMPLES OF SUBJECT BIBLIOGRAPHIES

Some examples of "Bibliographies" in specific subjects are:

ACM Guide to Computing Literature (a). 1964-. New York, Association for Computing Machinery

The guide 1990 is the 14th volume in the enhanced series of annual indexes. This volume indexes computing reviews, vol. 30-1990 annual lists an additional 22522 items. The guide contains seven sections; bibliographic listing; Author Index; Keyword index; Category index; Proper noun subject index; Computing Reviews; Reviwer index; and Source index. Each index contains the full title and sub-title of the work and a citation identification number indicating the location ranges. The bibliographic listing is divided into six sections: books, journals, proceedings, reports, doctoral theses, and computing reviews entry.

Aggrawal, Raj

International Business Finance; an annotated bibliography, N.Y. Praeger Pub., 1982 with index and cross references, inclusive through July 1978.

Basu, Kunal

Bibliography on the transfer of western management expertise to developing nations, (by functional area) Quebec Centre for Development Area Studies, McGill University, 1989. 1v. (various pagings)

This covered the period from 1983 - July 1988; having most recent 300 items with promising abstracts by functional area..

Cumulative Index to Sociology Journals - 1971-1985

Compiled by Judith Lantz. American Sociological Association, 1722, N. Street N.W. Washington, D.C. 20036, 1990.

ASA Sponsored publications are included. It has both an author and keyword subject index.

Entrepreneurship Development Institute of India

Entrepreneurship bibliography-II, Bhat, 1989. 44 p.

Environmental Periodicals bibliography. Bi-M.; 1972-. Environmental Studies Institute, Santa Barbala, CA, 93101-1552.

A current awareness bibliography featuring serial publications in the area of environmental studies.

Gupta, Anil K. and others

Inventory of peasant innovations for sustainable development; an annotated bibliography. CMA, IIM, Ahmedabad, 1990.

Gupta, Anil K. and others

Technology, farming systems research, environment, agriculture and rural development and related subjects; an annotated bibliography. 3v. CMA, IIM, Ahmedabad, 1989.

Based on Rural Development Abstracts, CAB, London, 1985-87.

Hyden, V.L

Management; A Selected Annotated Bibliography. Management Decision, Vol. 23, No. 1, 1985.

Hurey, Donnacadh, ed.

The management of technological change; an annotated bibliography. London, Intermediate Technology Publications, 1987.

Indian Council of Agricultural Research. New Delhi

Indian National Agricultural Bibliography 1975-84. 4v. 1987. New Delhi.

Covers the research work on Indian Agriculture over a period of 10 years from 1975-1984. It contains 38551 references from Indian and Foreign Journals Reports, Conferences, Proceedings, Technical bulletins, Books and Monographs on all aspects of agriculture, Forestry, Fisheries, Food, Rural development, Economics etc. The contents are classified into 85 subjects covering more than 950 commodities and products of animal and plant origin. It is highly useful to agricultural scientists, students, teachers, researchers, research management experts, information specialists and those who are engaged in agricultural research and development.

International Bibliography of Economics, 1952- (A)

International Committee for Social Science Information and Documentation. London, Tavistock Publications.

A classified bibliography of articles, pamphlets and books with author and subject indexes. It is a comprehensive survey on the economic literature.

International Bibliography of the Social Sciences. (Annual) (1952-.) Prepared on behalf of UNESCO by the International Committee for Social Science Information and Documentation. London, Routledge.

Published in four volume series of the bibliography are respectively dedicated to sociology. Economics, political science and social and cultural anthropology. Each of these volumes is intended to index the main primary publications of a given year pertaining to one social science discipline.The bibliography is international in its coverage and rest the most important publications in four disciplines. This bibliography is an essential working tool for researchers, University Arts Research institutions and librarians.

International Irrigation Management Institute, Library and Documentation Service

IMIN Bibliography; documents in the irrigation management information network (IMIN) database. Sri Lanka, 1987. 2v.

Jambhekar, A.; Pandya, J.F.; Shah, M.C. & Trivedi, G.J.

Social Forestry : A Literature survey (1975-1989). Ahmedabad, Indian Institute of Management, Ahmedabad, 1991.

Lbelle, R. Comp.

Agroforestry literature: a selected bibliography. Bomp. by R. Labelle and others. Nairobi, International Council for Research in Agroforestry, 1988. 269 p.

Management Bibliographies and Reviews. 1975- (Q) MCB University Press, England

Provides an uptodate information on new developments and thinking in management practice and serves as a invaluable resource for the research worker in practicing manager.

Pandya, J.F.; Shah, M.C. & Trivedi, G.J.

Energy; A classified bibliography - 1970-1985, New Delhi, Northern book Centre, 1991.

Close to 4300 references are listed in this bibliography. These references have been chosen from more than 200 journals, classified and placed under more than 85 different subject headings. It covers a comprehensive literature on all the important facets on the Indian energy scene and problems.

Pandya, J.F.; Shah, M.C. and Trivedi, G.J.

Studies in Indian Management; Annual Survey of Literature-1986. Ahmedabad, Indian Institute of Management, 1988. (Also published for the years: 1970, 1971, 1972, 1978).

Parikh, Indira J.

Women in management; an annotated bibliography with emphasis on commonwealth sources. Management Development Programmes. HRD Group, Commonwealth Secretariat, arlborough House, Pall Mare, London, SWJY 5HX.

Satyaprakash ed.

Agriculture: a bibliography. Guragaon, Indian Documentation Service, 1977.

The bibliography lists about 10,000 articles, research papers on agriculture from 172 Indian Journals covering the period 1962-1976.

INDEXING SERVICES

Indexing is a primary literature search since no one could possibly refer all the journals, papers published in various proceedings and conferences. The information required on any one topic may be scattered in many journals.

Articles are published in thousands in various journals and in various languages. Scanning such a large amount of literature is a stupendous task and would require enormous time. To facilitate quick and easy access to the information published in journals/periodicals indexes are very important tools.

These indexing service lists articles from a selected number of periodicals under chosen subject heading, and gives the full bibliographical reference for each article. They do not contain the summary of articles, but are very useful to the reader who wishes to read as much as possible on a particular subject as they provide references to many articles. The particular subject can be searched by using subject heading. Some such services in this field are given below:

Accountants Index; A Bibliography of Accounting literature (Q). Annual cumulation, (1921-). New York, American Institute of Certified Public Accountants.

A detailed index to books, reports, conference papers, sections from books, government publications, pamphlets and articles on finance and accounting. Arranged by author, title, and subjects in one alphabetical order. Annual volume includes more than 15000 references.

Applied Science and Technology Index. (Monthly except July) 1958- N.Y. H.W. Wilson

It is a subject index covering well over 391 journals in computer technology and application, energy resources and research, mathematics, food and food industry, plastics, textile, construction, transportation and other science and technology subject. It covers the major conferences and exhibitions. It has current book review and product reviews index separately.

Business Index (M) Information Access Company, Foster City, CA - 94404

Comprehensive guide to more than 700 business, trade and management journals including wall street journal' and the business finance section of the 'New York Times'.

Business Periodicals Index, 1958- New York, H.W. Wilson Co.

The American indexing service, which began in 1958, is the best available means of finding latest literature on business and industry.

The latest August 1988 - July 1989 annual volume of BPI has indexed about 310 periodicals. This index appears monthly, with quarterly and annual cumulations.

BPI is a cumulative index to English language periodicals. The main body of the Index consists of subject entries to business periodicals articles arranged in one alphabet. In addition, there is a separate listing of citations to book reviews following the main body of the index.

Subject fields indexed include accounting, advertising and marketing, agriculture, banking, building and buildings, chemical indudstry, communications, computer technology and applications, drug and cosmetics industries, economics, electronics, finance and investments, industrial relations, insurance, international business, management and personnel administration, occupational health and safety, paper and pulp industries, petroleum and gas industries, printing and publishing, public relations, public utilities, real estate, regulation of industry, retailing, taxation, transportation and other specific business, industries and trades.

Computer Literature Index (Q), 1971. Applied Computer Research, June, Phoemix, AZ - 85068

Bibliography of books, articles and reports relating to computers and data processing.

Guide to Indian Periodical Literature (Social Sciences and Humanities) (Quarterly/Annual). Gurgaon. Indian Documentation Service, 1964-.

The guide is a subject-author index to articles and other reading material appearing in about 500 Indian journals in the fields of social siciences and Humanities. The entries have been arranged alphabetically on the dictionary pattern.

Whenever possible, entries are made under "subject" headings. Headings are subdivided whenever the amount of material entered there warrants it and the nature of the material permits it. The two types of subdivisions used in the guide are (i) subheads (set in bold face type) and (ii) second subheads (set in light face italics). These subheads are also arranged in alphabetical order.

There are at least two entries for each article - an author entry and a subject entry except where there is no author. Additional subject entries have been made wherever the articles deal with more than one subject. The entries under subject headings are also arranged alphabetically. All related headings are covered by cross-references or by duplicate entries. The latest in the series is v. 24, published in 1987.

Index India: Jaipur, Rajasthan University Library, 1967-.

This outstanding index is a quarterly documentation list on India. It indexes nearly 460 Indian and 520 foreign periodicals. Entries in the index are arranged in classified sequence. An exhaustive alphabetical index to all possible subject headings is provided at the end. The headings are mostly derived through chain index procedure. Some important key-word out of context entries are also provided. Index India combines in the following one sequence (i) Indian Newspaper Index; (ii) Index to Indian Pieriodicals; (iii) Index to Foreign Periodicals; (iv) Index to Composite Publications; (v) Index to Biographical Profiles; (vi) Index to Book Reviews; (vii) Index to Theses and Dissertations; with separate Author and Subject Indexes.

Index of Economic Articles. USA, American Economic Association.

Each volume in the index lists articles in major economic journals and in collective volumes published during a specific year. Index volume covering 1969-1980 are available. Two part index volumes are available from 1981-1987, cover 100 year of economic literature indexed through 1886-1987 in 29 vols. is also available. The latest volume is 1988 published in 1992 (2 parts).

PAIS Bulletin, V. 74, (October 1987 - September 1988). New York, Public Affairs Information Service, Inc., 1988.

Public Affairs Information Service, Inc. is a non-profit association of libraries founded in 1914 for the purpose of indexing library materials in the field of public affairs and public policy.

The PAIS is a subject index in which each bibliographic entry appears under one to four subject headings in alphabetical order. PAIS aims to identify the public affairs information likely to be most useful and interesting to legislators, administrators, business and financial community, policy researchers and students. The PAIS indexes list publications on all subjects that bear on contemporary public issues and formation and evaluation of public policy, irrespective of source or traditional disciplinary boundaries. This includes the policy-oriented literature of the academic social sciences, economics, political science, public administration, international law and relations, sociology and demography, professional publications in the fields such as business, finance, law, education, and social work; and reports and commentary on public affairs from the serious general press. The listings encompass printed materials in all formats: periodical articles, books, government documents, and the reports of public and private organizations.

Business topics are extensively covered, with emphasis on economics factors,management policy making, business societal interactions and similarly other broad issues, rather than details of business operations.

About 1400 periodicals are scanned regularly for articles within the scope of PAIS. Books on subjects within the scope PAIS are listed selectively. Priority is given to books that are systematic investigations of specific policy issues which provide a comprehensive overview of positions and a range of approaches to a subject. Proceedings of a conference and symposia, reference books, statistical yearbooks, bibliographies, directories, handbooks and compendia of statutes are listed. Publications of national and state governments and inter governmental organizations are also listed.

Research Index. (Fortnightly). Wallington, Surrey. Business Surveys Ltd.

It includes articles and news items of financial interest appeared in about 150 business, news papers, economic and trade periodicals. Section 1 covers industrial, financial and commercial news, and section 2 covers company news arranged by name of companies.

It traces very recent information from newspapers like Financial Times, The Times, Wall Street Journal and from many business magazines.

SCIMP: Selective Cooperative Indexing of Management Periodicals-European Index of Management Periodicals. (1978-) (10 times a year)

It is an international European indexing service having a coverage of American and leading international journals. It indexes articles from 150 management periodicals having 6000 articles per annum, with a detailed author and subject index, circulated quarterly and annually.

Social Sciences Citation Index: (1973-) Philadelphia. Institute for Scientific Information. (3 year with annual cumulation)

A comprehensive indexing service covering more than 100 most important social science journals. It also includes business and management having citation index, permuterm-subject index and source index.

Social Sciences Index (Q). 1974-(Annual Cumulation) New York. H.W. Wilson.

Author and subject index to periodicals in the fields of anthropology, area studies, economics, environmental science, geography, law, political science, psychology, public administration, sociology and related subjects.

Vertical File Index. (Monthly except August). N.Y. H.W. Wilson Co.

The index offers subject access to the pamphlets covered, providing bibliographic information, ordering instructions and a descriptive note.

ABSTRACTING SERVICES

ISI standard defined abstracts "an abbreviated, accurate representation of the content of a document. It is usually accompanied by an adequate bibliographical description to enable the original documents to be traced. The primary purpose of an abstract is to help the users to decide whether the contents of the documents are such that they need to read it in full or not."

Abstracting services provide short abstracts of articles in a selected number of periodicals. Both abstracting and indexing journals include full bibliographical details such as the author's name, title of the article and the periodical reference i.e. name of the journal, volume No., issue No., date and pages. The abstracts are groups under different well selected subject headings. The abstracts are either indicative giving only brief summaries of the articles or informative giving the details of the articles. For this reason, the abstracting journals are more valuable than indexes.

All abstracts can be searched by using subject headings. There will be a separate subject index and the entries are arranged directly under subject headings. The subject headings used sometimes called index terms, search terms or keyword index. The users may have to think of possible synonyms for his search on the subject. It is also advisable to search more other abstracting services to ensure the adequate coverage of the subject.

Some of the "Abstracting Services" are listed areawise:

AGRICULTURE

Abstracts of Rural Development in the Topics. v.4; 1989. (Annual index) (Bi-M). Royal Tropical Institute, the Netherlands.

A journal offering approx. 2000 reference containing abstracts, subject index, geographical index, project index and author index.

Agriotech News and Information - CAB Abstracts, (Bi-M). UK CAB International Information Services.

It gives news, reviews and input from the CAB Abstracts, Database Abstract journals derived from the database of research on agriculture, forestry and allied disciplines, including social sciences and human machine. Abstract journals derived from the database, and online access to it, provide a unique source of information for research scientists, development planners, educators and students.

Agricultural Engineering Abstracts (M). 1976-. CAB International. Wallingford, Oxon, U.K.

Rural Development Abstracts. CAB International Information Services. Wallingford, Oxen, U.K..

It comprises about 2500 abstracts of documents concerned high rural development in the third world. The scope is broad and its coverage includes, agricultural and industrial production, investment, development projects, health, arid and women.

World Agricultural Economics and Rural Sociology Abstracts (M), 1959-. International Bureau of Agricultural Economics. CAB International Information Services, Wallingford, Oxon, U.K. It is an abstracts of World Literature.

COMPUTERS AND INFORMATION SYSTEMS

Computer Abstracts (M) Technical Information Co., Jersey.

An independent abstracting service in the field. U.S. Government research reports are also abstracted. Articles and papers in periodicals, confernece proceedings etc. are provided.

Computer and Control Abstracts (M). 1966- INSPEC, England.

Provides abstracts organised by subjects of international technological information.

Computer and Information Systems Abstracts (M). 1962- U.S. Maryland, Cambridge, Scientific Abstracts.

From programming to electronics, this journal provides complete coverage of research and applications in computer science. Aspects include artificial inteligence automation, system security, newly patented innovations and specific applications for any field of interest, from bio-medical and life sciencesto physics and engineering.

The journal contains about 17,600 abstracts per year. It has author/subject/acromym/nomenclature plus cumulative indexes.

Computing Reviews (M). Association for Computing Machinery, 11 West, 42nd St., St., New York, N.Y. 10036. The review aims to furnish computer persons in mathematics, engineering, the natural and social sciences, the humanities, and other fields with critical information about all current publications in any area of the computing sciences.

ECONOMICS

AID Research and Development Abstracts (Q). 1973-. Washington, Agency for International Development

Artha Suchi (Q) NCAER, Parsisila bhawan, 11 - Indraprastha Estate, new Delhi - 110 002.
An index to government reports, general articles and newspaper write-ups in the field of Indian economics which are being received in NCAER Library.

Asian-Pacific Economic Literature. 1987- (Half Yearly). March and September. Beach Tree Publishing, 10 Watford Chose, Guildford, Surrey, GUI 2EP, UK.
It is a reference work and research tool for all concerned with economic developments in the Asian-Pacific region. It regularly features literature surveys, abstracts of journals articles, contents list of journals, lists of working and other papers, book reviews and annotated list of books.

Economic Abstracts (Fortnightly) Martinus Nijhoff, The Hague. Includes abstracts on economics, finance, trade, industry, management, marekting, business and labour. Development Information Abstracts (Bi-M). 1981-New York, U.N. Dept. of Technical Cooperation for Development.
It provides rapid access to the studies, mission reports, and project reports generated by several offices of U.N.

Devinsa Development Information Network for South Asia. Abstracts: (Semi-Annual) (V.1-; 1987-) Sri Lanka, Marga Institute.
Devinsa was set up to develop a database of bibliographic information on socio-economic development in the South Asian Countries and to provide services from it. The

network presently covers Bangladesh, India, the Maldives, Nepal, Pakistan and Sri Lanka. Its main purpose to establish a network and creating a database to bring into bibliographic control unpublished literature produced in the South Asian Region on the broad area of social and economic development. The main focus is on the documents such as conference reports, reports to government and other development agencies, published and unpublished articles, theses, dissertations, research reports, working papers and technical reports.

ICSSR Journal of Abstracts and Reviews : Economics (Q). New Delhi. ICSSR, Lucknow, Giri Institute of Development Studies.

Each issue contains abstracts of selected articles in Indian economic periodicals, reviews of selected books including government reports, published in India.

International Development Abstracts (Q) 1982- England, Elsevier Science Publishers.
Covering all aspects of developing studies. It is an international abstracting service.

Journal of Economic Literature (Q). American Economic Association, Navshville, Tenn.
Includes annotated list of new books, classified by subject; subject index of articles in current periodicals with selected abstracts of more significant articles. It also gives contents for current economics journals.

Journal of Planning Literature 1986- (Q). Columbus, Olt. Ohio State University.

FINANCE AND ACCOUNTING

Accountants' Digest (Q). School of Accounting, College of Business and Public Administration, Florida Atlantic University, Boca Aaton, Florida, 33431.
The digest presents the outstanding articles selected from leading accounting journals of the English-speaking world.

Accounting and Data Processing Abstracts. London, Anbar Publication.
An excellent services in the field, critical comments are occasionally included. Annual Index contains abstracts of articles selected from 300 journals.

Accounting Articles (M). 1965- Chicago, Commerce Clearing House.
It is an impressive loose-leaf abstracting services carring periodical articles, books and pamphlets having indexes of topics and authors.

Journal of Foreign Exchange and International Finance (Q). Poona, NIBM.
The journal includes the section on "Annotated Articles".

MANAGEMENT

Anbar Management Services: Abstracts:London, AnbarPublications, 1961- (8 times a year).
Best British abstracting service. The service was divided in top management; personnel and training; marketing and distribution; accounting and data processing; work study & O and M with cumulative index.

Indian Management (M). New Delhi, All Indian Management Association.
Management Articles Referral Service is a quarterly service. Issue are slated to reach in January, April, July and October of every year.

International Executive (Bi-M). New York, American Management Association.
In each issue, the reference guide is listed and each item is listed under the headings for which the contents seem most pertinent. Short abstracts are given under the reference.

Management Abstracts. Digests and Reviews. (Q). London, British Institute of Management.
The abstracts are of high standard, often quite informative and cover many journals received in the BIM Library.

Management in Government (Q). New Delhi, Dept. of Administrative Reforms and Public Grievances.
The journal contains the abstracting section on Public Administration, Management etc.

Management Review. (M). N.Y. American Management Association.
It provides the digest of four articles of management interest each month.

Management Services and Production Abstracts (M). 1973- England. MCB Univ. Press. (Anbar Abstracts)
Contains abstracts of articles selected from 300 Journals.

Top Management Abstracts. London (8 issues), Anbar Publications.
Each issue contains abstracts of articles which cover all management aspects which are of interest to Senior Managers concerned with policy.

Smaller Business Management Abstracts (8 time a year) 1980-/ London, Anbar Publications.
It covers articles for small business, includes a classified contents and cumulative index.

Vikalpa; Journal of Decision Makers. (Q) 1976- IIM, Ahmedabad.
Abstracts of management research provide reference to articles based on Indian data and environment. Over 100 prominent journals published in India and abroad are scanned for the purpose. Empirical studies, experiences, ideas, and theories having a hearing on management in India are abstracted for this service, sponsored by ICSSR, New Delhi.

Wilson Business Abstracts. New York, H.W. Wilson Co.
Cover-to-cover abstracting of the 345 core business journals indexed in BPI. It is available on a disc having 1,30,000 expert abstracts having 57,000 subject terms for pinpoint accuracy. It is updated weekly.

MARKETING

International Packaging Abstracts (M). 1981-. Oxford, Pergamon Press.
Contains abstracts of publications and documents issued throughout the world relating to all aspects of packaging including commercial information. Each issue contains 350 references from international sources, among them 300 journals which regularly publish articles on packaging, including plastics, food and pharmaceutical journals. References are also taken from standards and specification, market reports technical reports, directions, books, government publications and of national press.

Journal of Marketing (M). Chicago, American Marketing Association.

'Marketing Literature Review' is published in all the issues of JM. This section is based on a selection of article abstracts from a comprehensive business literature database, marketing related abstracts from over 125 journals (both acadamic and trade) are reviewed by JM staff.

Management & Marketing Abstracts (M). 1976-; Oxford, Pergamon Press.

Management and marketing academics and executives need to know the latest developments in management thinking and practice. The journal keeps readers abreast of development by regularly scanning over 200 major business journals, conference proceedings, reports and selected items of interest, arranged under 25 separate headings having an index. It provides an uptodate surveillance of the world's specialist literature in this area.

Marketing and Distribution Abstracts (M). 1971- London, Anbar Publications

It contains the abstracts of articles selected from 300 journals in the field of marketing, advertising, stock control, distribution, transport and warehousing.

Market Research Abstracts (SA). 1963- NTC Publications, P.O. 69, Henley-on-Thames, Oxan, U.K.

Covers all fields of marketing and advertising research as well as relevant papers in statistics, psychology, economics, sociology and other fields relevant to market researchers.

ORGANIZATIONAL BEHAVIOUR

HRD Documentation Bulletin. 1988- (Q). United Nations Development Programme and ILD, Asian Employment Programme (ARTEP).

It provides computerised information regarding books, reports and articles on human resource planning and related subjects. For easy subject searching, key word and author Indices with corresponding serial number of entry are provided at the end of the bulletin.

ICSSR Journal of Abstracts and Reviews: Sociology and Social Anthropology. (Bi-Annual).

It contains abstracts of researches in the field of sociology and social anthropology and allied disciplines.

Indian Psychological Abstracts (Q). New Delhi, ICSSR.
It contains abstracts of psychological literature produced in Indian and also includes the doctoral works on India.

Psychological Abstracts (M) American Psychological Association, Arlington, VA.
It includes the world's journal literature in psychology and related behavior and social sciences. Each monthly issue includes citations with information, non-evaluative summaries from English language journals and technical reports. At the end of the year Author and Subject indexes are published to provide access to the years literature.

Social Planning, Policy and Development. Abstracts. (S-A) 1979-. San Diego, CA, Sociological Abstracts.

Social Work Research and Abstracts (Q) 1965-. MD. Association of Social Workers.

Sociological Abstracts (Q). N.Y. Sociological Abstracts Inc.
More than 800 periodicals are regularly scanned and more than 8,000 abstracts are classified under 29 main headings. It has a very comprehensive coverage. For management section 0600-coupled organisations (Management) may be consulted.

PERSONNEL AND INDUSTRIAL RELATIONS

Human Resources Abstracts (Q). London, Sage Publications.
HRA covers human, social and manpower problems and solutions ranging from slum rehabilitation and job development providing to compensatory education, minority group problems, and rural poverty. This is a service of information to researchers in the diverse area of poverty, manpower and huaman resources development.

Personnel and Training Abstracts (8 issues a year). 1971-London, Anbar Publications
Contains the abstracts of articles selected from many journals, on the subject.

Personnel Management Abstracts (Q). Chelsea, Michigan, PMA.
An annotated subject list of recent articles on the management of people and organizational behaviour from a large number of academic and trade journals. It also contains abstracts of selected books.

Work Related Abstracts, Harnumic Part Press, 23620, Pinewood, Warren, Michigan, 48091.
Includes human behaviour education and training, eoconomics; socio-economic and political issues.

Work Study and O and M Abstracts (8 issues a year) 1971- London, Anbar Publications.
Contains abstracts of articles selected from many journals on the subject.

PRODUCTION AND QUANTITATIVE METHODS

International Abstracts in Operations Research (Bi-M). International Federation of Operational Research Societies by Elsevier, North-Holland.
The journal provides abstracts of papers published in the field of OR. Each year, about 2400 abstracts are included, which give a comprehensive guide to the current OR literature. Over 150 journals from all over the world and of all languages are regularly being screened by reviewers.

Mathematical Reviews (M). 1940- American Mathematical Society, Providence, RI 02901-9930.
A reviewing journal covering the world literature of mathematical research.

OR/MS - Operational Research/Management Science (M). U.S.A. Executive Sciences Institute, Devenport, Iowa.
It is an international literature digest alerting about the availability of the original articles.

Statistical Theory and Methods Abstracts (Q). International Statistical Institute, Edinburgh.
Gives abstracts of papers with contributions to the theory and natural of multinational statistics; theory of probability and related subjects. It also includes relevant research reports and reports of conferences, seminars and symposiums.

PUBLIC SYSTEMS

Abstracts of AIT Reports and Publications on Energy, (A). Asian Institute of Technology, Regional Energy Resources Information Books. Bangkok 10501, Thailand.
The purpose is to made known the documents resulting from research carried out at the AIT in the field of rational use of energy, energy and renewable energy resources. The document listed comprise of theses, research reports,

conference proceedings, and periodical articles, and are cited with abstracts to give our readers in idea of the scope and results of the completed research projects. Keyword and author indexed are provided.

Documentation in public Adminsitration (Q). New Delhi, IIMA.
Abstracts material on various aspects of public administration, makes ordinance to management and allied subjects, and brings out an index of articles appearing in daily newspapers.

Energy Abstracts (M). 1974- Engineering Information In. New York, N.Y. 10017.
Abstracts of the world's literature in the field of energy.

Energy Digest (Bi-M). New Delhi, TERI
Each issue comprises of 110 abstracts and 4-5 extended summaries and digest, nearly 500 journals and other sources such as conference proceedings, technical reports, books etc. are regularly scanned.

Energy Information Abstracts. (M). 1976- Bowker A & I Publishing, New York, N.Y. 10011.
Focuses on research and development, resources, consumption, conservation, economics, and industrial application of energy sources and technologies. Information is abstracted and indexed from scientific, technical, and business journals, conference and symposium proceedings; and academic, government, and corporate reports, includes a listing of conferences and events.

Energy Management (Q). New Delhi, National Productivity Council
In each issue the section on 'Energy Abstracts' is given

Environment Abstracts (M). 1970- Bowker A & I Publishers, New York, N.Y. 10011.
Addresses the impact of human-kind and technology on the environment with attention to air, water, and noise pollution, solid and toxic wastes, radiological contamination, toxicological effects, control technologies, resource management, population, endangered species, and geographical and climatic changes. Information is abstracted and indexed from scientific, technical, and business journals; conference

and symposia proceedings, newsletters, and academic and government reports. Includes a listing of conference and events.

Environmental Resources Abstracts (Q). New Delhi. World-wide fund for nature.
The first part 'Environmental Abstracts' presents abstracts of articles/reports largely from professionals publication. The second part Media aleart on Environment and Devleopment Abstracts items relevant to environment.

Fuel and Energy Abstracts. (Bi-M). London. Institute of Energy, London, Butterworths.
It comprises of comprehensive coverage of the latest world literature relevant to all technical, scientific, commercial

ICSSR Journal of Abstracts and Reviews: Political Science (Bi-Annual). New Delhi, ICSSR.
The journal publishes abstracts of articles, book reviews, list of reviews published in Journal of Political Science and Allied Disciplines.

Paryavaran Abstracts; 1984- (Q). Environmental Information System (ENVIS) Dept. of Environment, Forests & Wildlife, Paryavaran Bhavan, CGO Complex, Lodi Road, New Delhi - 110003.
It reports current Indian Literature on environmental sciences. Abstracts have been directly taken from source documents like primary periodicals, research reports, seminar proceedings, standards and patents. Reviews and informatic articles contributed by subject specialists are also included.

Resources in Education (M). Washington, D.C., Educational Resources Information Centre.
A monthly abstracting journal announcing recent report literature related to the field of education, permitting the early identification and acquisition of reports of interest to the educational community. ERIC is a nationwide information network for acquiring, selecting, abstracting, indexing, storing, retrieving, and disseminating significant and timely education-related reports.

Sage Public Administration Abstracts (Q). London, Sage Publications, 1991-

The PA Abstracts is an international information service that gleans the most significant new literature from public administration and related literature like 'Developing Countries' 'Economic Development and Policy' 'Information Trade', Research Methodology etc. etc. This easy-to-use resource brings concise abstracts of literature from 250 selected sources.

RESEARCH SOURCES: RESEARCH COMPLETED OR RESEARCH IN PROGRESS

For a researcher, it is very important to know what other relevant research has been or is being carried out by other researchers in his/her field. Reviewing of literature in the field is very time consuming as there is no comprehensive source available. Researchers in business and management areas generally want to know new developments and ideas. There are many forms of publication such as doctoral thesis and dissertations; discussion and working papers, conference papers and proceedings; research reports. There are publications issued by business schools, university departments; research groups or units; government departments and agencies, independent research bodies and sometimes by banks, stock exchanges, trade unions and professional bodies. The publications published by the above stated agencies are important because these report the result of current research, new ideas and to some extent leads to important developments which are very useful for the researcher point of view. Many universities and business schools have published their own list of thesis. But unfortunately not all research is documented for general access. However, there are few important reference sources which lists:

i) **COMPLETED RESEARCH SOURCES**

The information about completed research is available in the form of books where these are listed or in the journals where a section is devoted for such information.

ii) A list of journals according to the subjects listed below, in which research articles; research studies and research notes are being published. regularly - is given in the following pages.

1. Agriculture
2. Computers and Information Systems
3. Economics
4. Finance & Accounting
5. Management
6. Marketing
7. Organizational Behavior
8. Personnel & Industrial Relations
9. Production & Quantitative Methods
10. Public Systems

DISSERTATIONS - BOOKS

Abstracts of Doctoral theses accepted for award of Ph.D. degrees during the period from January 1, 1985 to December 31, 1985 and January 1, 1986 to December 31, 1986. New Delhi, Jawaharalal Nehru University, 1986 and 1987. 438 p.

Abstracts of Fellow Programme in Management - Dissertations (1984-1990): Ahmedabad, IIM, 1991.

This is the fourth book-let in the series includes abstracts of 47 theses accepted during the period 1989-90. The subject areas covered by the dissertations are varied and wide ranging covering topics such as management of technology, operational planning for road transport corporations and irrigation projects, consumers behaviour, organizational change, corporate financial decisions, industrial relations systems, and economic behaviour of industries. The booklet would be found useful by researchers, professionals and practioners in management.

Abstracts of Students Projects in Management 1983-1987: 2v. Narsee Manjee Institute of Management Studies.

V.1 -Marketing, Finance, Operations Research and Personnel

V.2 - Perspectives, Bombay 1988.

ACM Guide to Computing Literature. v. 14; 1990. New York, Association for Computing Machinery.

The bibliographic listing is divided in five sections, books, journals, proceedings, theses, and computing reviews extras. This 1990 edition lists about 440 theses submitted to the American Universities. Author, Title, name of the University and University Microfilms International order is also given, so that the theses can be procured easily.

American Doctoral Dissertations (Annual). Ann Arbor. University Microfilms 1964/65-
Covers American and Canadian University theses. Arranged under index subject headings and institutions having no abstracts.

B.H.U Research Profile; Documentation of Doctoral Dissertations upto 1980, ed. by S.N. Raghow and others. Varanasi, Banarasi Hindu Univ. 1986
The profile encompasses entire gamut of intellectual pursuit from its very inception to 1980. The total title covers 3355.

Bibliography of Doctoral Dissertations : 1986-87. Social Sciences and Humanities. New Delhi, Association of Indian Universities, 1990.
The bibliography lists 2815 doctoral dissertations in the disciplines of Social Sciences and Humanities accepted by Indian Universities during 1986-87. An alphabetical subject index and a scholar index are included.

A Bibliography of Doctoral Dissertations Accepted by Indian University 1957-1970. New Delhi, Inter-University Board of India and Ceylon, 1972-1975. 4v.
Contents: v.1. Social Sciences; V.2. Humanities.- v.3 Biological Sciences; v.4. Physical Sciences.

Bibliography of Published Research of the World Employment Programme. 9th ed. Geneva, ILO, 1991.
ILO Publications and works divided into books and reports and articles in International Labour Review and Working Papers. All entries are listed in geographical and chronological order within their respective categories. The bibliography contains an author index and a country and area index. List all WEP Publication and documents produced between 1981 and March 1991.

Catalogue of Theses and Dissertations, 1950-1969. Pune, Jayakar Library, University of Pune, 1971.
It lists 1548 titles on all disciplines.

Compendium of Research, 1951-1976, ed. by M.S. Chennaveeriah and others., Dharwar, Karnataka University, 1976.

Comprehensive dissertation Index. 1861-1972, Ann Arbor, Michigan, University Microfilms International, 1973. 37 v. The CDI data base also offers computerised service called DATRIX-II. It prepares cumulative inter-disciplinary listings of dissertations in any field on request. Covers American doctoral dissertations over the period 1861-1972. Annual Supplements are issued.

DBA Theses Abstracts (A). Boston, Graduate School of business Administration, Harward University.

Harward DBA Theses are listed. (Unpublished).

Disserations in Economics: 1921-1971: Abstracts of M.A. and Ph.D. Theses, ed. by C.H. Shah and D.T. Lakdawala. Bombay, Department of Economics, University of Bombay, 1974. 672 p. (University of Bombay Publications, Economic Series, no. 22). Golden Jubilee Publication, Bombay, Population Prakashan, 1979.

Doctoral Students in Social Sciences - 1969. 2 parts. Delhi, Inter University Board of India and Ceylon and ICSSR This contains information about students registered for a doctorate degree in social sciences in Indian Universities as on 30th September 1969, and contains 2988 entries. Author, guide and subject index is provided.

Doctorates in Social Sciences Awarded by Indian Universities upto 1967. New Delhi, Inter University Board of India & Ceylon and ICSSR, 1971 ICSSR has already published two volumes of Doctorates in Social Sciences awarded by Indian Universities in the year 1968 and 1969. The present volume covers the theses in social sciences awarded by Indian Universities since their inception upto December 1967. It includes entries for 1849 theses from 43 universities and Institutions. The author index, guide index and the subject index is given.

Documentation of Doctoral Theses in Economics in the Banaras Hindu University 1943-1967. Varanasi, 1969.

Economics, Commerce, Management; a Bibliography of Doctoral Dissertations Accepted by Indian Universities. 1857-1970. New Delhi. Inter-University Board of India.

Economic Research of Interest to Agriculture: 1988-1990. California, University of California, Division of Agriculture and National Resources, 1991.
It represents the research activities of the Agriculture Economists Group in the California Agricultural Experiment Station and the California Cooperative Extension Service. The list serves not only as a record of published and unpublished materials but also as a reference guide to source materials in the area of agricultural and resource economics research.

European Doctoral Theses in Management: Bibliography. Brussels European, Institute for Advanced Studies in Management

ICSSR Research Projects 1969-1988: A list of Research Projects Sanctioned since the inception of the ICSSR to March 1988, New Delhi, ICSSR, 1990.
The council has been giving grants to scholars for conducting research in various social science disciplines in India. Till March 1988, a total of 1837 research projects were sanctioned by the council. Author Index, Subject Index and State Index is given at the end for easy consultation.

Index to Theses Accepted for Higher Degrees in the Universities of Great Britain and Ireland, London, Aslib, 1950/51.
Lists theses by broad subject, with author index and no abstract.

Indian Dissertation Abstracts Index. Vol. 1-10; 1973-1981. Journal. New Delhi, NASSDOC.

List of Theses Accepted for the Award of Ph.D. Degree Closing the years 1960-1978. Vallabh Vidyanagar. Sardar Patel University.

Marketing Doctoral Dissertations. (Annual). USA. American Marketing Association.
It lists more than 70 dissertations a year from about forty American Universities.

National Register of Doctoral Dissertations Accepted and in Progress in Social Sciences and Humanitics in Social Sciences. Bhopal, Council for Oriental Research, 1979-80. It covers Economics and econometrics in Vol. 1, Vol. 1-B contains agricultural economics; v.2 - Public Administration; v.4 - Sociology, and V.5, Commerce, business administration .and management; Indian and Personnel Administration, and Psychology in Vol. 8.

Post-Graduate Theses Abstracts 1980. Coimbatore, Tamil-Nadu Agricultural University, 1981.

Register of Development Research Projects in Asia and Far East Paris, OECD, 1989.
The register contains information on 847 research projects in one field of economic and social development carried out by the member countries of ADIPA in 15 countries of Asia-Pacific region.

Register of Development Research Projects in Latin Americaa. Paris, OECD, 1984
The two volumes on Latin American contain detailed information on 436 research and training institutes which are located in 25 countries at the continent and on 1739 current research projects carried out in these countries.

Research in Progress ; a Record of Subjects Taken up for Research by Scholars Registered for Doctoral Degrees with the Indian Universities during 1958-66. New Delhi, Inter- University Board of India and Ceylon. 1968-72. 4v. Contents: v.1. Physical Sciences; v.2. Biological sciences; v.3. Social Sciences; v.4. Humanities.

Research in progress - A record of subjects taken up for research by scholars registered for doctoral degrees with the Indian Universities during 1958-66. V.3 - Social Sciences. New Delhi. Inter Univ. Board of India and Ceylon, 1970.
This volume deals with the social sciences and lists 1311 research projects initiated during 1958-66

Selected list of U.K. Theses and Dissertations on Management Studies. (Annual). U.K. British Business School Librarians Group.

Social Sciences - A Bibliography: Doctoral Dissertations accepted by Indian Universities : 1857-1970. New Delhi, Inter University Board of India, 1974.
For the first time information about doctoral theses, Ph.D., D.Sc., D.Phil. accepted by Indian Universities has been collected. Subjectwise lists are also being brought out in paperbacks. This volume dealing with the social sciences has been published first of all. It lists 2819 theses by Indian Universities for doctoral degrees. A scholar index and an alphabetical subject index are included.

Social Science Research in South Indian Universities; a Listing and Review of Ph.D. Dissertations, by Madras Institute of Development Studies and ICSSR Regional Centre, Hyderabad, 1989.
This publications listed about 1476 Ph.D. theses completed in 18 Universities in the region. The list gives the name of the candidate, the title of the theses, name of the University and the year of the award of degree.

Synopsis of Doctoral Theses in Social Sciences, 1955-1975, Dharwar, Karnataka University, Dharwar, 1978.

University Research in Business and Economics; a bibliography. Bureau of Business Research. West Virginia University, College of Business and Economics. W. Verginia.
The annual lists books, working papers, series, articles in journal published by various business institutes, arranged by subject, name of the Institutions, and the author index.

DISSERTATIONS - JOURNALS

A few following academic journals in management related areas list abstracts of accepted theses.

American Economic Review. (Q). U.S. American Economic Association.

The December issue of each year contains a list of American dissertations in economics arranged in 10 subjects. Two sections cover : "Business Administration"; "Industrial Organization and Public Policy".

American Economist.
Spring Issue.

American Journal of Agricultural Economics. U.S. American Agricultural Economics Association.

Ph.D. Recipients by Subject in May issue each year.

Business Horizons. Bloomington. Graduate School of Business. Indiana University.

Each Issue contains the thesis.

Dissertation Abstracts International - A. The Humanities and Social Science. (M). An Arbor, University Microfilms.

Dissertation Abstracts International (DAI) includes abstracts of Doctoral Dissertations submitted to UMI by nearly 500 participating Insititutions in North America and throughout the world.

Each author-prepared abstract, upto 350 words in length, describes in detail the original research project upon which the dissertation is based. Most of the approximately 30,000 dissertations published by UMI each year are abstracted in DAI and may be purchased in microform or as paper copies. Entries are grouped by author-selected subject. Within each subject category, entries are arranged alphabetically by author.

All bibliographic data relating to a dissertation appear at the Head of an entry. The abstract then follows. Each entry contains the following essential research information; Title; Author's name; Degree and date earned; Institution granting the degree; Number of pages in the original dissertation; reference to location of abstracts in DAI; and UMI Order Number.

There are 3 Sections. Section B deals with the Science and Engineering, Section C - European Abstracts, is published quarterly and includes abstracts of dissertations in area disciplines accepted for doctoral and post-doctoral degrees at European Institutions.

Economic Journal (Q) 1981.Cambridge. Royal Economic Society.

Since 1971 the March issue of each year has 'Thesis' titles for Degrees in the U.K.', arranged by subject.

Finance India. (Q) Delhi, Indian Institute of Finance.

The journal has a regular section on 'Abstracts of Doctoral Dissertations'.

ICSSR Newsletter (Q). NASSDOC, New Delhi.

Lists 'Research Projects' completed/in progress published/unpublished; doctoral fellowships, published dissertations and research reports.

ICSSR Research Abstracts (Q) New Delhi, ICSSR.
It publishes abstracts of reports funded by the ICSSR. The object is to disseminate the findings of research work in the field of social sciences as quickly and as widely as possible.

Index India. Jaipur. Rajasthan University Library.
Index India has a section on 'Theses and Dissertations' in each issue. It list the theses submitted to the Indian Universities arranged in a broad subject group.

Indian Dissertation Abstracts (Q) 1973-. New Delhi, ICSSR and Association of Indian Universities.
The journal carries abstracts of research theses in the social sciences on which Ph.D. degrees were awarded by the Indian Universities. The abstract contains a write-up on the problem; the methodology and the major findings.

Indian Journal of Industrial Relations. (Vol. 1, No. 2; October 1965; pp. 231-237).
List of doctoral theses in industrial relations approved by the Indian Universities during 1960-63.

Industrial and Labour Relations Review. Ithaca, N.Y. New York, State School of Industrial and Labor Relations.
Research in Progress in each issue.

Industrial Relations Journal (Q). Oxford, Blackwell.
Each issue contains 'Research Note'.

Industrial Relations Theses and Dissertations. (A). Ann Arbar, Michigan University Microfilms International.
Compiled from Dissertation Abstracts online database onwards. Theses on industrial relations area arranged by more than 60 subject headings.

Journal of Business (Q). Illinois, Graduate School of Business. University of Chicago, Chicago.
January issue lists the American doctoral dissertations accepted arranged in 18 broad business subject areas. January 1990 issue lists for the year 1988-89.

Journal of Creative Behaviour, Buffalo, N.Y. Creative Education Foundation.
Bibliography of recent Doctoral Dissertations on Creativity and problem solving in fourth quarterly issue.

Journal of Economic History. Iowa city, Iowa, Economic History Association.

Summaries of 'Doctoral Dissertations' in June issue.

Journal of Economic Literature (Q). Nashaville, Tenn. American Economic Association
Designed to provide economists with a guide to ongoing research and publications includes index of articles on economic subjects.

Journal of Finance, N.Y. American Finance Association
March Issue lists Abstracts of completed dissertations in the field of "Economics" and "Business Finance".

Journal of International Business Studies. Academy of International Business and University of South Carolina.
"Dissertation Abstracts" in each issue.

Journal of Operations Management. (Q) Columbia, Missouri, Univ. of Missouri - Columbia, College of Business and Public Administration.
Each issue has section on: "Dissertation Abstracts".

Journal of Retailing. N.Y. University Institute of Retail Management.
'Dissertation Reviews' in Summer issue.

Masters' Abstracts (Q). Univ. Microfilms.
It gives brief abstracts of selected masters and other theses available from the publishers.

Omega: The International Journal of Management Science. Oxford, Pergamon Press.
International Register of Theses and Dissertations in each issue.

Opsearch (Q). Delhi, Operations Research Society of India.
Each issue of the journal contains abstracts of doctoral theses in operations research submitted to Universities in India.

Research Abstracts (Q). Univ. Microfilms.
It lists brief, abstracts of selected masters and other theses available from the publisher.

Theses Abstracts 975 (Q). Hissar. Haryana Agricultural University.
Abstracts of doctoral theses approved for degrees by the various agricultural universities and National Institutes in India.

University News. (W) New Delhi. Association of Indian Universities.

i) A section 'List of research scholars registered in Indian Universities' is given in each issue.

ii) A section 'Theses of the month' in which a list of doctoral theses accepted by the Indian Universities is given in each issue.

University Research in Business and Economics. (A).

College of business and Economics, West Virginia University.

Work Related Abstracts

It includes relevant entries from Dissertations Abstracts International.

ANNOTATED SELECT LIST OF JOURNALS HAVING RESEARCH ARTICLES, RESEARCH STUDIES & RESEARCH NOTES (SUBJECT-WISE)

AGRICULTURE

Agribusiness. (Bi-M). New York, John Wiley & Sons.

The journal serves the community of researchers and practitioners in industry, academia, and government who deal with the broad spectrum of the business of agriculture including agricultural inputs, agricultural production, commodity processing, food manufacturing, and food distribution. It also examines the coordinating mechanisms among the sectors of the food and fiber system such as pricing systems, government policy and facilitating institutions. It provides a single forum for agribusiness related papers - especially those of an applied nature.

Agricultural Economics Research Review. (Half yearly) 1988- New Delhi, Agricultural Economics Research Association, IARI.

Articles and research notes on basic and applied research on economic aspects of agriculture and rural development are published.

Agricultural Situation in India (M). India. Ministry of Agriculture, Delhi, Controller of Publications

The journal has now established itself as research journal in agricultural economics, including policy making, planning and research.

Agricultural Systems (M). (incorporating Research and Development in Agriculture). U.K. Elsevier Science Pub. Ltd.

An international journal presents the results of studies

concerning the whole or parts of the food chain from production to consumption

Agriculture and Human values (Q). Gainesville, Agriculture, Food and Human values Society, Univ. of Florida.
It is an interdisciplinary journal for educators, researchers, policy makers and research managers who have an interest in understanding the implications of alternative food and agricultural policies and practices. The journal seeks to create educational and scholarly junctures between liberal arts and agricultural disciplines.

American Journal of Agricultural Economics (5 years). U.S. American Agricultural Economics Association.
Each year May issue contains the list of Ph.D' Recipients by subject with Institution index. A list of Awardwinning thesis is included in the issue of December 1989.

Australian Journal of Agricultural Economics (3 issues a year).
The Journal provides an outlet for creative work in agricultural and applied economics.

European Review of Agricultural Economics (Q). Walter de Gruyter & Co., Pastfash (10240, D-100, Berlin-11 FRG).
The review serves as a forum for discussions about the development of theoretical and applied agricultural economics research in Europe and for stimulating ideas regarding the economic problems of agriculture in Europe and other parts of the world.

Indian Journal of Agricultural Economics (Q). Indian Society of Agricultural Economics, Bombay.
The objective of the journal is to provide a forum for dissemination and exchange of findings of research on agricultural economics. Includes 'Research Notes' also.

Journal of Agricultural Economics Research (Q). Rockville, M.D. ERS-NASS, U.S. Dept. of Agriculture.

Journal of Agricultural Engineering Research (M). Academic Press, USA on behalf of British Society for Research in Agricultural Engineering.
This is a wide and reflects the interdisciplinary nature of Agricultural Engineering Research. It includes all aspects of mechanization and buildings of relevants to field crops horticulture and livestock.

Journal of Rural Development (Bi-M). National Institute of Rural Development, Hyderabad - 500 030.
It aims at promoting study and research in rural development.

Journal of Rural Studies (Q). Pergamon Press, Headington Hill Hall, Oxford, U.K.
The journal is a forum for the publication of research articles relating to such rural issues as society, demography, housing, employment, transport, services, land- use, agriculture and conservation. Particular emphasis is on planning, policy and management

Rural Sociology (Q). Rural Sociological Society, Department of Sciology. Montma State University, Bozeman, MT 59715.
The journal promote the development of rural sociology through research, teaching and extension work. The issues contains the "Research Notes'.

COMPUTERS AND INFORMATION SYSTEMS

Computers and Operations Research (Bi-M). Oxford, Pergamon Press
The journal provides an international forum for the application of computers and operations research techniques to ecology, transportation, safety, realiability, urban planning; economics; inventory control; investment strategy and military analysis and related fields. It ensures its maximum utility to all researchers, teachers, and practitioners interested in oprations research, computer and their applications.

Computers in Human Behavior (Q). 1985- Oxford, Pergamon Press.
It is a scholarly journal dedicated to examining the use of computers from a psychological perspective. Original theoretical works, research reports, literature reviews, software reviews, book reviews and announcements are published.
The journal includes articles dealing with the psychological effects of computers on phenomena such as human development, learning, cognition, personality and social interactions. The primary message of most articles involves information about human behavior.

Computer in Industry; an International Journal. The Netherlands, Elsevier Science Publishers, In.

The aim of the journal is to stimulate further cross industrial research, development and implimentation of computer applications in industry. The journal contains articles on the use of computer aids in decision making, formal project specification, design, manufacturing production in small medium and large-sized industrial enterprises. It gives special attention to practicles addressing quality, interfacing and integration, and to polydiscipline solutions.

Information and Management, Systems, Objective, Solutions, 1978- (10/yr). Elsevier Science Publishers, Netherlands.

For managers of information systems, researchers and systems designer, provides information on new developments in applied information systems.

Information Processing and Management. (Bi-M). U.S.A. Pergamon Press.

The journal is devoted to referred reporting of: basic and applied research, communication, cognitive science, and related areas, that deals with the generation, organizaiton, storage, retrieval, transfer and utilization of information; the nature, manifestation, and effects of information, knowledge and communication; and human information behavior.

Information and Software Technology (M). Oxford, Butterworth- Heinemann Ltd.

An international technical journal covering software development. It provides up-to-date information on the latest software development research.

Journal of computer and System Sciences (Bi-M). N.Y. Academic Press, Inc.

The purpose is to publish original research papers in computer science and system science with emphasis on the relevant mathematical theory and its applications.

Journal of Systems Management (M). Cleveland, JSM.

JSM covers the tools, technology and techniques of successful business information systems management through its case studies, editorials and in-depth articles - all written by leading business professionals.

ECONOMICS

American Economic Review (Q). American Economic Association, U.S.
The December issue of each year contains a list of American dissertations in economics arranged in 10 subjects having sections on 'Business Administration' and "Industrial Organization and Public Policy"

Anvesak. (2/yr). Ahmedabad, SPIESR
It publishes the research work undertaken by the staff of the Institute.

Asian Development Review (2/yr). Manila, Asian Development Bank
Asian Development Review is aimed at encouraging economic research and analysis to bring about a deeper understanding of the dynamics of the development process. It contains discussions on major development issues, the results of research carried out by bank staff, and contributions from scholars and specialists concerened with Asian and Pacific Affairs.

Economic Journal (Q). Royal Economic Society of U.K. Cambridge, England.
Since 1971 the March issue of each year has 'Thesis titles for Degrees in the U.K.', arranged by subject.

Industrial Researcher (Q). Pranava Industrial Societies, 18, Sagar Tarang, B.D. Road, Bombay - 400 036.
This is a journal of research on industry. Journal provides detailed information on current status, exports, imports, estimated demand, names of manufacturers and performance of the industry in last 10 to 15 years.

Journal of Economic History (Q). Economic History Association, Iowa City, Iowa. U.S.A.
June issue has "Summaries of Doctoral Dissertations".

Journal of Economic Literature (Q). American Economic Association, 2014, Broadway Suite 305, Nashville, TN 37203.
It gives the list of doctoral degrees conferred by American Universities. It contains the contents of current periodicals; subject index of articles in current periodicals; selected abstracts; and doctoral dissertations in economics.

Journal of Economic Theory (Q). Academic Press Inc., 1250, Sixth Avenue, San Diego, CA 92101, USA.
The Journal publishes original research on economic theory and emphasizes the theoretical analysis of economic models, including the study of related mathematical techniques.

Journal of Economics and Business (Q). Elsevier Science Publishers, The Netherlands.
The Journal provides a prominent forum for scholarly research in applied economics, finance and related business disciplines that focus on the domestic and international aspect of business and society.

Journal of Forecasting. (Bi-M). 1982- U.K., John Wiley & Sons
The journal is well established as a prestigious research oriented journal committed to reporting new theories and practices across a broad spectrum of disciplines and applications. Focussing on model-building for forecasting the journal strongly features-relevant technical material from, statistics; econometrics; systems engineering and judgemental psychology.

Journal of Housing Economics. 1991-. USA, Academic Press Inc.
The journal provides a focal point for the publication of economic research to housing. The journal provides a broad coverage like international comparisons; impact of the local public sector and construction industry studies

Journal of International Development: Policy, Economics and International Relations (Q). New York, John Wiley &Sons, Published for the Institute for Development Policy and Management.
The purpose of the journal is to make quickly available the fruits of development-related research.

Margin (Q). NCAER, Parisila Bhavan, 11, Indraprastha Estate, New Delhi - 110 002.
It is designed primarily to publish contributions on applied economic problems researched by NCAER's own staff. It had a section on 'Project Completed Recently' and 'Projects-in-hand at NCAER'.

Oxford Bulletin of Economics and Statistics (Q). England, Basil Blackwell.

It publishes international research papers on current practical issues in applied economics for academic and professional economists worldwide in both the privàte and public sector. It publishes research papers in all areas of applied economics.

Progress in Planning. (Bi-M) (2 vol. a year). Oxford, Pergamon Press.

It provides rapid publication of extended papers drawn from recent research in planning. A wide range of interdisciplinary interests is covered including sociology (and in particular urban sociology) economic urban, rural, transport and population geography demography, environmental studies, socio-economics, transportation, highway and traffic engineering, social sciences and administration, operational research, research and development, long-range planning and technological forecasting, computer and management information systems and management studies.

Regional Science and Urban Economics (Q). North-Holland, Elsevier Science Publishers, BV

The journal encourage high quality scholarship on important theoretical and empirical issues in urban and regional research. The journal focus emphasis on microeconomic analysis of spatial phenomena. The journal solicits original research contributions in spatial economics, economic geography, and reputed disciplines. The journal encourage the submission of theoretical and empirical contributions related to market organization in space, housing, and labour markets, transportation and local public economies.

Review of Business and Economic Research. 1965- (2/yr). University of New Orkans, College of Business Administration, New Orleans, LA 70148.

Review of Economic Studies (Q). C/O Tieto Ltd., 108, Courley Road, Oxford, U.K.

The object of this review is to encourage research in theoretical and applied economics

Social-Economic Planning Sciences; the International Journal of Public-Sector Decision Making (Q). Oxford, Pergamon Press.

It provides a medium for research either because of the interdisciplinary or applied character of the study or the mathematical/quantitative nature of research, dealing with decision problems in the service and public sectors.

World Bank Economic Review. 1987-. (3/Yr). Washington, World Bank

It is a professional journal for the dissemination of World Bank sponsored research which informs policy analysis and choices.

World Development (M). Oxford, Pergamon Press

It is a multi-disciplinary international journal devoted to the study and promotion of world development. It provides original research and review articles devoted to the social, economic and political consequences of development when used as a means to eliminate the chief evils of the world today: malnutrition, disease, illiteracy, poverty, poor living conditions and unemployment.

World Economy (Q). Trade Policy Research Centre, 11 Grosvenor Crescent, London, SWIX TEE

The journal aims to promote independent research and public discussion of international economic policy issues and focusses on the conduct of international economic affairs.

FINANCE AND ACCOUNTING

Accounting and Business Research (Q). London, The Institute of Chartered Accountants in England and Wales

It is a publication of substantial and original contributions to knowledge in the areas of accounting and finance

Accounting Review (Q). U.S. American Accounting Association- Includes research notes on current research projects in the field of accounting (January issue).

Applied Financial Economics (Q). London, Chapman & Hall, (v.1-; 1991-)

It published research papers, short articles, notes, comments on financial economics, banking and monetary economics, with a particular bias towards practical aspects and applied topics. It is important reading for financial economists, financial institutions, economists in banks and specialist in accountancy, management and economics.

Finance India. (Q). Indian Institute of Finance. P.O. Box, 8486; Ashok Vihar, Delhi - 110 052.

The primary aim of the journal is to provide research by disseminating the results of such research in finance, accounting and related areas. It is intended to provide scholars a major forum for disciplinary and inter-disciplinary study of various aspects of finance. The journal publishes articles, research papers, contents and abstracts of articles published in different journals, recently published and an extensive bibliography on one of the areas related to finance.

Financial Management, 1972-(Q). FMA, University of South Florida, College of Business. Tampa, Fl. 33620.

Presents research papers and analysis on the economic aspects of operating a corporation, focussing on markets, stocks, financial leverage, pricing, trading, purchase/lease options, and cash-flow, with news brief on the latest developments in the field.

Indian Journal of Finance and Research (Bi-M). IJFR. 116-D, Packet IV, Mayur Vihar, Delhi - 110 001.

It publishes articles on finance, portfolio management, theretical and empirical analysis in corporate finance and allied fields.

Journal of Accounting Research (Semi-Annual). Illinois, Graduate School of Business. Univ. of Chicago.

Contains 'Research Reports' on the subject.

Journal of Accounting and Finance (Bi-Annual). Jaipur, Research Development Association.

It is academic and research journal in the fields of accounting, business, mathematics, taxation and finance.

Journal of Business Finance and Accounting. Basil Blackwell, 108, Cowley Road, Oxford, OX4 1JF, UK.

The journal aims to advance the academic understanding and professional practice of effective financial management, control and accountability by publishing research of high quality, based on theoretical or empirical analysis.

Journal of Finance (5 times). American Finance Association. New York Univ. N.Y.

(March Issue). The quarterly publishes abstracts of completed dissertations in the field.

Journal of Financial and Quantitative Analysis (Q). Graduate School of Business Administration. University of Washington. DJ-10, Seattle, WA 98195. USA.
The journal publishes theoretical and empirical research in financial economics. Topics include corporate finance, investments, capital and security markets and quantitative methods of particular relevance to financial researchers. It further advances research in finance.

Journal of Financial Economics (Published in 3 Vols, 6 issues a year). Elsevier Science Publishers, North Holland
The journal intends to provide a specialized forum for the publication of research in the general area of financial economics, planning primary emphasis on the highest quality analytical mathematical and empirical contributions in the following major areas; consumption and investment decisions under uncertainty, portfolio analysis, theories of market equilibrium, the dynamic behaviour of asset prices in the financial and real sectors and the concept of 'efficient markets', relationship between the financial and real sectors, and normative theory of financial management.

Journal of Financial Research 1978- (Q).
Arizona State University, College of Business, Department of Finance. Temple. AZ 85287-3906.

Journal of Foreign Exchange and International Finance (Q). International Finance, Pune, NIBM
The journal provides a forum for debate and discussion of high quality theoretical and empirical research in the areas of foreign exchange and international finance. It also provide an outlet, for research in evaluation and interpretation of innovations in the instruments and techniques of international finance and foreign exchange markets. It also includes the section on 'Annotated Articles'.

Journal of International Financial Management and Accounting. (3 times a year). Basil Blackwell, 108 Cowley Road, Oxford, IJF? U.K.
The journal publishes original research dealing with the international aspects of financial management extending

into banking and financial services, accounting, auditing and taxation.

Journal of Money, Credit and Banking (Q). Ohio State University Press, Ohio, USA.
The journal is a primary economics journal reporting major findings in the study of monetary and fiscal policy, credit markets money and banking portfolio management and related subjects. It is widely read and cited by researchers and policy makers.

Journal of Portfolio Management (Q). N.Y. Institutional Investor.
Well researched articles, many by academicians to exchange the latest ideas in portfolio management.

Journal of Risk and Insurance (Q). Department of Finance, College of Business Administration, University of Central Florida. Orlands, Florida, 32816.
The journal is multidisciplinary publication, with primary emphasis on high quality research leading to feature articles, shorter articles and comments on wide variety of risk, insurance and risk management topics.

Review of Quantitative Finance and Accounting (Q). 1991-. Norwell, Kluwer, Academic Publishers.
The journal deal with research involving the interaction of finance with accounting, economics and quantative methods.

MANAGEMENT

ASCI Journal of Management (Q). Hyderabad, Administrative staff College of India.
The papers are based on research work, and consulting and professional experience. It also publishes 'research notes'.

Academy of Management Journal (Q). U.S. College of Business Administration, Univ. of Oregon
The journal publishes only original, empirical research as articles or research notes. It also publishes reports of research that develops, tests or advances management theory and practice. September issue of the journal contains 'Research Notes'.

Administrative Science Quarterly (Q). Graduate School of Business and Public Administration, Cornell University

ASQ is a multi-disciplinary journal dedicated to advancing the understanding of administration through empirical investigation and theoretical analysis. The emphasis is on research articles.

Australia Journal of Management. (2 issues in Vol.). Australia. Australian Graduate School of Management, Univ. of New South Wales

The objectives are to encourage and publish research in the field of management. It publishes research in applied economics, finance, industrial relations, political science, psychology, statistics and other disciplines, provided the application is to management as well as research in areas such as marketing, corporate strategy, operations management, organization development, decision analysis, and other problems - focussed paradigms.

British Journal of Management (Q). (New Journal from 1990), England, John Wiley & Sons.

It aims to provide an outlet for research and scholarship on management oriented themes and topics.

Decision. (Q) Calcutta, Indian Institute of Management.

A forum for original and thought provoking papers based on applied research in management and social sciences

Harvard Business Reveiw (Bi-M). Graduate School of Business Administration, Harvard Univ.

A scholarly journal with an emphasis on research articles covering all reports of business and other related topics.

Executive (Q). Academy of Management Executive. Ohio Northern Univ., Ohio.

The primary goal of the 'Executive' is to provide protecting executives with relevant management tools and information based on resent advances in management theory and research.

iimb Management Review. (2 issues a year). Bangalore, Indian Institute of Management

The journal focusses on management applications and public policy.

Indian Journal of Public Enterprise. (Q). 1986- Institute of Public Enterprise Research, Allahabad

It promotes, provides and enlarging facilities for research in public enterprises and allied subjects

Indian Review of Management and Future (Q). 1977- A-3, Pandala Road, New Delhi - 110 003.
A journal of advanced learning in administration and management.

International Executive (Bi-M). New York, John Wiley.
It aims at advancement and dissemination of research in the field of international business.

International Journal of Management and Systems (3 issues a year).IJOMAS, 16, Vaishali, Pitampura, Delhi-110034.
It publishes research papers with emphasis on quantified approach and application to management problems, computer science, statistics systems science, operational research, social sciences and other related areas.

International Small Business Journal (Q). U.K. Woodcock Publications.
Each issue contains "Research Note".

Journal of Business (Q). Illinois, Cambridge Graduate School of Business, University of Chicago, Chicago.
January issue lists the doctoral dissertations accepted arranged in 18 broad business subject areas. January 1990 issue lists for the year 1988-89.

Journal of Business Research (8 times a year). Elsevier Science Pub. co., N.Y.
The journal applies theory developed from business research to actual business situations. It examines a wide variety of business decisions, processes and activities within the actual business setting. It aids the applications of empirical research to practical situations and theoretical findings to the reality of the business world.

Journal of Economics and Business (Q). Pennsylvania, Temple University, Philadelphia
The journal is devoted to professional and academic research in economics, finance, management, marketing and related disciplines.

Journal of Entrepreneurship (Q). Ahmedabad Entrepreneurship Development Institute of India
It covers research, evaluation and innovative programme in the fields of entrepreneurship and regional development. The journal is of interest to national, state and rural planners, geographers, educationalists, researchers and others involved in entrepreneurship and

the micro-economics of regional development in advanced and developing countries.

Journal of General Management (Q). Henley - The Management College, Oxfordshire, England
The journal aims to foster new thinking, research and the exchange of experience between academics and policy makers on an international basis.

Journal of Institute of Public Enterprise (Q). Osmania University Campus, Hyderabad - 500 007
The journal is devoted to professional and academic research on the economics and management aspects of public sector enterprises.

Journal of International Business Studies (Semi-Annual). Academy of International Business and the University of South Carolina.
"Dissertation Abstracts" are listed in each issue.

Journal of Management; an International Journal of Management Research (Q). College of Business Administration, Texas; ACM University college Station, USA.
The journal publishes original research articles related to the study of management and organization.

Journal of Small Business Management (Q). College of Business and Economics, West Virginia Univ. Morgantown, USA.
It publishes high quality articles, research notes and other features in the fields of small business management and entrepreneurship.

Long Range Planning (Bi-M). Oxford, Pergamon Press
LRP has become recognised worldwide in the leading journal in the field of strategic planning includes enhanced international coverage. The journal provides an indispensible source of information on current developments and new thinking about the problems and techniques of forward planning in business and government. The journal include industry and market analysis. Strategy formulation and implementation, company cases from large and small business, the facts and techniques for strategic planning, strategies for growth and in declining materials, and the use of

information technology in planning. With the inclusion of a current awareness service, review and current articles LRP is the essential reference for senior managers in industry, corporate planners, management consultants, administrators in government, and academics and researchers of strategic planning and strategic management.

Journal of Strategic Information Systems (Q). 1982- Oxford, Butterworth-Heinemann
The journal welcomes papers from both academics and practitioners on research into the evaluation and application of information technology for strategic purposes. The focus of the journal is on the management business, and organizational issues associated with the introduction and utilisation of information systems as a strategic tool.

Journal of the Society and Research Administrators (Q). Chicago
Publishes a variety of articles intended to expand the knowledge and tools of research administration.

Management in Government (Q). New Delhi, Dept. of Administrative Reforms and Public Grievances
The journal provides a forum for all. practising administrators and others interested in research, training and practice in public management.

Management Research News. (8/yr). Barmalickk Publications, England.
Provides precise, informative and reliable accounts of management research.

Prabandh. (MBA Programm) (Bi-annual). Udaipur, Department of Business Administration. Sukhadia University
The Journal is devoted to professional and academic thinking and scholarly research in the field of management. It has a section on micro-researches which present abstracts of project reports of MBA participants.

Sloan Management Review. MIT, Sloan School of Management, Cambridge, MA 02139.
It provides the practicing manager with the latest tools and information needed for effective problem solving and decision making. Articles discuss new techniques, case

studies, models and research trends of practical significance to the professional manager.

Small Enterprise Development (Q). U.K. Intermediate Technology Publications

The journal aims to provide a forum for those involved in the design and administration of small enterprise programmes in developing countries. It contains detailed articles reporting original research, important field experience and significant new developments.

Strategic Management Journal (Bi-M). New York, Wiley.

The journal publishes original material concerned with all aspects of strategic management. It publishes communication in the form of research notes or comments from readers on published papers or current issues.

Vikalpa; The Journal for Decision Makers (Q). 1976- Ahmedabad, Ineian Institute of Management

Vikalpa publishes a wide range of articles and papers based on experience and research on managerial problems in business and industry, agriculture and cooperatives, and government organizations. The articles and the special feature 'Diagnostic' which presents a case are rich in implications for managers, administrators, and policy makers for examination and analysis. Abstracts of management reaches in India are presented to facilitate research in management. Vikalpa is a premier management journal researches to the corporate world, public administration, development agencies, non-profit organizations and researchers, teachers and students of management.

MARKETING

European Journal of Marketing. 1967- (10/yr). MCB University Press Ltd., 62, Toller Lane, Broadford, West Yorkshire, BD8 9BY, England.

Presents the practical applications of new ideas and developments in marketing research, covers market planning, customer policy and service, marketing of services, history of advertising, and product development.

Findex - Worldwide Directory of Market Research Reports, Studies and Surveys. (Semi-Annual) 1984-

Findex indexes and summaries over 11,000 market research reports commercially availabe worldwide. Information includes consumer studies, surveys, audits and company reports in 90 industries, with subject areas ranging from defense and security system to health care.

Industrial Marketing Management (Q). N.Y. Elsevier Science Publishing Co.

It presents innovative concepts and strategies in areas like; product and market planning; forecasting; sales management, buyer behavior; market research; and product management. It is an invaluable source for scholars and practitioners who want to remain uptodate on the latest developments in organizational marketing.

International Journal of Research in Marketing (Q). Elsevier Science Publishers, B.V. (North-Holland) P.O. box 1991, 1000 BZ Amsterdam, Netherlands

IJRM aims to contribute to the body of knowledge about research in marketing by performing an integrative function, publishing theoretical and empirical articles from all countries and with different disciplinary approaches. It covers the entire area of marketing. It provides a high quality medium through which both developments in marketing theory and thought and results of empirical research can be communicated to those entire in marketing research as well as those wishing to be performed about progress in the field.

International Marketing Review, (5/yr). England, MCB Publications

It provides a forum for academics and practioners to consider the latest developments and advances in knowledge and practice of international marketing.

Journal of Advertising Research. (Bi-M). Advertising Research, 40 Foundation, U.S.

The journal is intended for practitioners and users of advertising research.

Journal of Consumer Research (Q). University of Chicago Press, Chicago, IL 60637.

Covers marketing, psychology, anthropology, and economics with a focus on academics rather than managerial. Topics range from micro level processes, such as brand choice, to more macro-level issues, such as the development of materialistic values.

Journal of International Marketing and Marketing Research. 1976- (3/yr). European marketing association, 18 St. Peters steps, Brixhem, Devon, England

Journal of Marketing (Q). American Marketing Association, 2505, Wacker Drive, C Chicago Il 60606.
Each issue has 'Marketing Literature Review' which is based on a selection of articles abstracted from a comprehensive business literature database. Marketing related abstracts from over 125 journals are reviewed. The abstracts are available on line from the ABI/INFORM database.

Journal of Marketing Research (Q). American Marketing Association, Chicago.
Covers methodology and problems of research in marketing, discusses current trends and experiments in social psychology and other behavioural sciences as they affect marketing.

Journal of the Market Research Society (Q). Market Research Society, 175, Oxford St., London, WiR 1TA
This is a leading professional journal of marketing research worldwide, and publishes authoritative original contributions to both the theory and the practice of market research and to stimulate discussion and future research effort.

Journal of Retailing (Q). New York University. Institute of Retail Management
Summer (formerly sprint) issue contains several "Dissertation Reviews". It keeps informed about new research findings, concepts, methods and challenging inquiry in the field. Includes research notes.

Marketing Letters; a Journal of Research in Marketing. Kluweh Academic Publishers, Worwell, MA 02061
It is a journal of research focusses on empirical findings, methodological papers and theoretical and conceptual insights in the field of marketing. It publishes the most uptodate information and the newest trends in marketing.

Marketing Research (Q). 1989- Chicago, American Marketing Association .

This is a new practical publication exclusively for marketing researchers

Market Research (Annual). London, Arlington Publications Ltd.
Directory of 18,000 published market research studies. Each study listing includes, title, a brief summary, countries worked, page, price, date of publications and author reference.

Psychology and Marketing (Q). John Wiley & Sons, 605, Third Avenue, New York, N.Y. 10158
The journal publishes original research and review articles dealing with the application of psychological theories and techniques to marketing.

ORGANIZATIONAL BEHAVIOUR

American Sociological Review. (Bi-M). American Sociological Association, 1722 N. Street, N.W., Washington, D.C. 20036.
The review publishes work of interest to the discipline in general, new theoretical developments, research that advance and understanding of the most fundamental social process, and important methodological innovations. Each issue contains 'Research Notes'.

Communication Research (Q). Sage Publications, California.
Research articles are published in four regular issues per year that significantly advance the theoretical involvement understanding of human communication processes.

Creativity Research Journal (Q). New Jersey. Ablex Publishing corporation.
The journal publishes high quality, scholarly research capturing the full range of approaches to the study of creativity: behavioral, clinical, cognitive, cross-cultural, developmental, educational, genetic, organizational, psychoanalytic and psychometric. Interdisciplinary research is also published.

Human Relations (M). New York, Plenum Publishing Corporation
The journal discusses theoretical developments, present new methods, or review articles, as well as report empirical research. The journal intent to reflect a broad spectrum of problems and approaches towards an integration of the social sciences.

Human Resource Management (Q). N.Y. John Wiley & Sons, Inc.
The journal provides both the business and research communities with insights to help guide organizational transitions into the 1990s.

Human Resource Management Review (Q). 1991-. Connecticut, Jai Press Inc.
It publishes conceptual/theoretical articles pertaining to human resource management and allied fields (e.g. industrial/organizational psychology). Its purpose is to provide a forum for ideas that will promote and lead research as well as for the critical examination of existing concepts, models, and frameworks, subject areas include but are not limited to personnel selection, compensation, performance appraisal, retention, training and development, human resource management applications of computer techology, and human resource planning.

Indian Journal of Psychology (Q). IJP., 27-A Masjid Moth (viii) New Delhi - 110 049.
The journal publishes original research as well as the theoretical papers and research notes.

Indian Journal of Social Science (Q). Sponsored by ICSSR, New Delhi
It promotes scientific discussion on the diverse concerns of social science research - the problems of development and social change, the interface between science, society, culture and technology, and development as they relate to the developing countries.

International Journal of Contemporary Sociology (Bi-Annual). Dept. of Sociology University of Joensuu, Finland.
A discussion journal of contemporary ideas and research. It publishes the findings of both quantitative and qualitative research. Emphasis of theory as well as applications of the principles of sociology.

International Journal of Organizational Analysis (Q).
Dept. of Management, Western Kentucky University. Bowling Green, KY 42104, USA. (To be published in January 1993)

International Journal of Psychology. (Bi-M). Elsevier Science Pub., Amsterdam, netherlands.

The journal emphasis basic research and theory rather than technical and applied problems. It is devoted to scientific and theoretical papers in all fields of psychology.

Journal of Applied Social Psychology (M). 7961, Eastern Avenue, Silver Spring, MD 20910.

The journal disseminates findings from behavioural science research which have applications to current problems of society.

Journal of Behavioral Decision Making (Q). 1988- England, John Wiley & Sons.

It is a multidisciplinary journal with a broad base of content and style. The objective of the journal is to present and stimulate behavioral research on decision making and to provide a forum for the evaluation of complementary, contrasting and conflicting perspectives. These perspectives include: psychology, management science, sociology, political science and economics. A major forum for research in decision making.

Journal of communication (Q). N.Y. Oxford University Press

The journal is concerned with the study of communication theory, research practice and policy. It is for those in every field who are interested in research and policy developments and in the public impact of communication studies.

Journal of Creative Bahaviour (Q). Creative Education Foundation, Bulfala, N.Y.

'Bibliography of recent Doctoral Dissertations on Creativity and Problems-Solving' is appeared in the fourth quarterly issue of each year.

Journal of Experimental Social Psychology. (Bi-M.). Academic Press, 1250, Sixth Avenue, San Diego, CA 92101, USA.

It publishes original research and theory on human social behaviour and related phenomena. Research areas include: attitude and belief processes, inter-group and inter-group processes; social cognition, social interaction and social motivation.

Journal of Organizational Behaviour (Bi-M). John Wiley *\& Sons, England

It aims to report and review the growing research in the industrial/organizational psychology and organizaitonal behaviour fields throughout the world. The 'Research Notes' is included in all the issues of the journal. Original article are sought that advances the knowledge of applied behaviour analysis in work and organizational setting.

Journal of Social Policy (Q). Cambridge, Cambridge University Press

'Research note' is published in some issues

Organizational Behaviour and Human Decision Processes (Bi-M). Academic Press Inc., 1 East First Street, Duluth, MN 55802

It is a journal of fundamental research and theory in applied psychology. It publishes papers describing original empirical research and theoretical developments in all areas of human performance theory and organizational psychology.

Personnel Psychology; a Journal of Applied Research (Q). USA 9660, Hillcroft, Suite 337, Houston.

The journal publishes empirical applied research dealing with a wide range of personnel problems facing public and private sector organizations. Articles with all aspects of personnel psychology including employee selection, training and development job analysis, productivity important improvement programmes, work attitudes, labour management relations, and compensation and reward system. Critical state-of-the-art reviews of the research literature in these areas are also published.

Rural Sociology (Q). Rural Sociology Society, Montana. State Univ. Montana.

Promoting the development of rural sociology through research, teaching and experiment work. The journal includes 'Research Notes' and a Special Feature.

Small Group Research (Q). London, Sage Publications.

It presents research, theoretical advancements and empirically supported applications with respect to all types of small groups.

Social Forces, (Q). University of North Carolina Press, Box - 2288; Chapel Hill. North Carolina, 27515-2288.

It is an important international journal of social research.

Social Science Research (Q). N.Y. Academic Press

A journal of social science methodology and quantitative

research. It publishes papers on quantitatively with substantive issues in all social science areas and with social science methods.

Social Research. (Q). N.Y. New School of Social Research.

Sociological Methods and Research (Q). London, Sage Publications.

A leading journal of quantitative research and methodology in the social sciences.

PERSONNEL AND INDUSTRIAL RELATIONS

British Journal of Industrial Relations (Q). Oxford, Basil Blackwell Ltd.

It is a journal of research and analysis covering every aspect of industrial relations in Britain and overseas. It publishes empirical and theoretical papers on industrial relations topics, broadly defined. These can include any aspect of the industrial relations system including the operation of industrial relations institutions, trade union issues, management and analysis of industrial relations outcomes.

Indian Journal of Labour Economics. (Q). A.N. Sinha Institute of Social Studies, Patna - 800001.

The journal includes 'Research Notes'. Promote Scientific Studies in Labour Economics.

Industrial and Labour Relations Review (Q). New York State School of Industrial and Labour Relations, Cornell University, N.Y.

Having a section on 'Research in Progress' in each issue.

Industrial Relations: (3 times a year). Institute of Industrial Relations, Univ. of California, Berkeley.

It publishes articles on all aspects of employment relationship, shorter papers are considered for Research Notes Section.

International Labour Review, (Bi-M). ILO, CH-1211, Geneva-22 (Switzerland).

Articles based on recent ILO and other research into economic and social topics of international interest affecting labour.

Journal of Labour Economics (Q). Chicago, Univ. of Chicago Press.

It includes articles on labour economics, labour markets and demographics, unions and collective bargaining. Compensation and benefits distribution of income, applied and policy issues. It's international research examines issues affecting the economy as well as social and private behavior. And by serving as a forum in which labour economists share their data and techniques of analysis. It helps in identifying new methods to further your research.

Journal of Labour Research (Q). Department of Economic George Mason. Univ. Fairfax, Virginia 22030.
Focuses on policy issues related to trade unions including their political and economic activities.

Journal of Managerial Psychology. (Q) England, MCB Univ. Press Ltd.
The journal provide all these involved in managerial psychology with uptodate ideas, new research on major issues and current case studies for the development of people at all levels in organisations.

Labour and Society (Q). Geneva, ILO.
Contains articles on social and labour problems as well as an account of the current educaional and research activities of the International Institute for Labour Studies.

Management and Labour Studies (Q). Jamshedpur, Xavier Labour Relations Institute
The journal focusses the latest thinking and research in the areas of management, labour and related subjects.

Personnel Review, 1971. (5/yr.) Institute of Personnel Management); MCB University Press, England.
Seeks to present the latest research and developments in all disciplines of relevance to the personnel specialist.

PRODUCTION AND QUANTITATIVE METHODS

IIE Transactions: Industrial Engineering Research and Development (Q). Georgia Institute of Industrial Engineers
It aims to foster a rich interchange among researchers in the field and practitioners, and to propagates these ideas to the entire industrial engineering community. This includes the 'Technical Note' also.

International Journal of Production Economics. The Netherlands, Elsevier Science Publishers

The journal focues on topics treating the interface between engineering and management. It is interdisciplinary in nature, considering whole cycles of activities such as the product of life cycle - research, design, development, test, launch, disposal - and the material flow cycle - supply, production, distribution.

Journal of Engineering and Technology Management (Q). 1972–. The Neatherlands, Elsevier Science Publishers

The journal aims to promote the theory and practice of technology and engineering management. The journal links engineering, sciences and management disciplines. It addresses the issues involved in the planning, development, and implementation of technological capabilities to shape and accomplish strategic and operation objectives of an organization. It covers not only R & D management, but also the entire spectrum of management concerns in technology-based organizations.

Journal of Operations Management (Q). University of Missouri-Columbia. College of Business and Public Administration Middlebush Hall, Columbia, Missouri 65211.

The mission of the journal is to publish original, high quality research in the field of operations management.

Journal of Product Innovation Management (Q). New York, Elsevier Science Pub. Co.

The Journal is dedicated to the advancement of management practice in all the functions involved in the total process of product innovation. It presents the research, experiences and insights of academics, consultants,practising managers, Economists, Scientists, lawyers, sociologist. Articles are based on empirical research, well considered observations of management experience, and state-of-the-art reviews of important issues as well as conceptual and theoretical developments.

Journal of Purchasing and Materials Management (Q). National Association of Purchasing Management, Tempe, Arizona

The journal publishes articles which are analytical in nature and discuss theories, principles and applications; and report relevant research which contribute to the advancement of knowledge in the various areas of purchasing materials management and related fields.

Journal of the Operational Research Society (M). Birmingham, The Operations Research Society Ltd.

The journal presents paper which are relevant to practitioners, researchers, teachers, students and consumers of operation research and which cover the theory, practice, history or methodology.

Mathematics of Operations Research (Q). Institute of Management Sciences Providence, RI.

It publishes significant research and review papers having substantial mathematical interest and relevance to operation research/management science.

Networks (Q). New York, John Wiley & Sons

The journal publishes original research papers, significant results of design efforts, and tutorial papers covering technological or mathematical disciplines. It also publishes material on the theory and design of the full gamut of networks as well as techniques used to study them. Among these are results from mathematical programming, combinatories, reliability theory, graph theory, probability theory, statistics, queueing theory and computer programming.

Omega : The International Journal of Management Science (Bi-M). Oxford, England and Elmsford, N.Y.

Each issue contains "Intenrational Register of Theses and Dissertations" - Omega reports on developments in management including the latest research result and applications. It is an important source for practising managers, specialists by management services, operational research markets and management scientists, management consultants, academics, students and research personnel.

Operations Research (Q). Operations Research Society of America

Publishes quality OR and management science work of interest to the OR practitioners and researchers.

Operations Research Letters (Bi-M). Operations Research Society of America. Netherlands, Elsevier Science Publishers

The Journal is a novel and innovative publications for the literature on all aspects of operations research and the management and decision sciences.

Production Planning and Control (Q). (Vol. 1-1990). Taylor & Francis, London

PPC is a quarterly international journal with two main aims, first to bring together research papers on all apsects of PP&C and provide a medium for the rapid publication to all researchers specializing in PP&C and secondly, to create a better understanding between researchers and management in industry by providing articles on industrial applications, new techniques and development trends.

Productvity (Q). New Delhi, National Productivity Council

It presents the results of original research and analysis. It disseminates information on concepts of data on productivity and its growth in India and elsewhere.

Statistical Science. (Q). California. Institute of Mathematical Statistics.

The aim is to present the full range of contemporary statistical thought at a technical level accessible to the broad community of practioners, teachers, researchers, and students of statistics and probability. The journal publish discussions of methodological and theoretical topics of current interest, surveys of substantive research areas with promising statistical applications.

Technology Studies. 1992- Berlin. Walter de Gruyter

It will bring together research, critical analysis and proposals devoted to the study of technological innovation, change, work processes, adaptation, the quality of work life in a technological environment and the role of technology in society. The major aim of the journal is to ensure broad perspectives on technology studies and to provide forum for diverse viewers from various disciplines.

PUBLIC SYSTEMS

Energy Management (Q). New Delhi. National Productivity council

The journal is devoted to dissemination of Information on recent developments, technological innovations, R & D activities etc. in the field of energy management and conservation

Energy Policy. (10 times a year). U.K., Butterworth Heinemann Ltd.

The journal addresses the .economic, environmental, political, planning and social aspects of.energy supply and utilization which confront decision makers, corporate planners, managers, consultants, politicians and researchers.

International Journal of Energy Research. 1976- (6/yr). John Wiley & Sons, Sussex P019 IUD, England.

Journal of Communications (Q). New York, Oxford Univ . Press

The journal is concerned with the study of communciation theory, research practice and policy. It is addressed to those in every field who are interested in research and policy developments and in the public impact of communication studies.

Journal of Policy Analysis and Management (Q). New York, John Wiley & Sons

JPAM strives for quality, relevance, and orginality. It gives priority to articles that relate their conclusions broadly to a number of substantive fields of public policy or that deals with issues of professional practice in policy analysis and public management. It also publishes articles that review the state of knowledge in particular policy areas.

Journal of Public Economics. (3 volumes). Netherlands, Elsevier Science Pub.

The aim is to encourage original scientific contributions on the problems of public economics with particular emphasis on the application of modern economic theory and methods of quantitative analysis. It provides a forum for discussion of issues of public policy of interest to an international scholarship.

Local Government Studies. (Q). London, Frank Cass.

The journal seeks to provide a forum in which academics and those engaged in local government policy making and management can exchange information and ideas.

Optimum; the Journal of Public Sector Management (Q). Canada, Univ. of Ottawa

It aims to build a dialogue among practitioners, researchers, academics and students on the leading edge of public sector management. While its focus is on management and the public sector, it seeks original materials of relevance from all sectors, including articles on private sector management and practice that have applicability to the public sector. It publishes both theretical and applied materials that deal with current and future trends in the practice of public sector management.

Policy Sciences (Q). The Netherlands, Kluwer Academic Publishers.

It is an international journal devoted to the improvement of policy making. It gives articles which examine the normative aspect of policy sciences and conceptual article which address concrete policy issues.

Public Administration (Q). Oxford, Basil Blackwell.

The journal aims to publish articles which will stimulate both scholarly and practitioner interest in public administration.

Public Administration and Development (Q). England, John Wiley & Sons.

It is an international journal of training, research and practice. It reviews and assesses the practice of public administration at local, regional and national levels where this is directed to development in developing countries.

Pacific and Asian Journal of Energy. (Half Yr). 1991- New Delhi, Tata Energy Research Institute

PAJE covers the latest developments in the field of energy studies as these relate to energy policy and resource planning. Senior researchers policy makers, and administrators are encouraged to share their experiences, innovations and views.

Public Administration Review. (Bi-M). American Society for Public Administration, 1128 G Street, N.W. Washington, D.C., 10005.

It publishes timely material based on research pertinent to the interests of the board spectrum of public administration.

Regional Development Dialogue. Japan, U.N. Centre for Regional Development.
The journal seeks to provide a forum for critical discussion of regional development problems, policies, and perspectives among academicians and practitioners. It addresses particularly to policy makers, government officials, professional planners, and members of academic community.

Transportation Research; Part A - General. Pergamon Press, New York
"Recent Doctoral Dissertations" published in each year in the first issue of the journal.

ACADEMIC PERIODICALS

Academic periodicals which are directly emanating from business schools and academic and research institutions have greatly contributed to the development of new concepts, practices and theories in the field of management and economics. The output of these periodicals is the input for generating new knowledge and information. These journals are being subscribed by many such libraries and their articles and references are being cited in number of books, journals, thesis, and project reports by the researchers. A list of such selected Indian and Foreign Journals is given below:

ASCI Journal of Management. (2/Yr). Hyderabad. Administrative Staff College of India.

Academy of Management Journal. (5/Yr). Ohio Warthern University. Ada. Oh.

Administrative Science Quarterly (Q.). Graduate School of Business and Public Administration at Cornell University, Mallot Hall, Cornell University. Ithaca.

Business. (Q) Atlanta, Georgia State University.

Business and Society (Q.). Chicago, College of Business Administrates, Roosevelt University.

Business History Review. (Q.) Boston, Harvard Business School.

Business Horizons. (Bi-Monthly.) Bloomingston, Graduate School of Business, Indiana University.

Business Quarterly. (Q.) School of Business Administration. University of Western Ontario.

California Management Review. (Q.) Graduate School of Business Administration. University of California, Berkeley, California.

Columbia Journal of World Business. (Q.) Graduate School of Business Administration. New York, Columbia University.

Decision. (Q.) Calcutta. Indian Institute of Management.

Entrepreneurship Theory and Practice. (Q.) Waco, School of Business, Baylor University.

Financial Management. (Q.) Tampa, College of Business Administration. University of South Florida.

Harvard Business Review. (Bi-monthly). Graduate School of Business Administration, Harvard University, Boston.

Human Resource Management (Q). School of Business Administration, University of Michigan. Published by John Wiley & Sons.

iimb Management Review. (2/Yr). Bangalore, Indian Institute of Management.

Industrial and Labour Relations Review. (Q.) Ithaca, NY, Cornell University.

Journal of Accounting Research. (Semi-Annual). Chicago Graduate School of Business, University of Chicago.

Journal of Business. (Q.) Chicago, Graduate School of Business. University of Chicago.

Journal of Consumer Research. (Q.). Provo, UT, Graduate School of Management, Grigham Young University.

Journal of Contemporary Business (Q.). Graduate School of Business Administration, University of Washington, Seattle.

Journal of Finance. (5/Yr). New York, Graduate School of Business, New York University.

Journal of Financial and Quantitative Analysis. (Q.). Seattle, Graduate School of Business Administration. University of Washington.

Journal of International Business Studies (3/Yr). Columbia University of Carolina, College of Business Administration.

Journal of Macromarketing. (Semi-Annual). Graduate School of Business Administration. University of Colorado, Colorado.

Journal of Management. (Q) college of Business Administration. Texas A&M University.

Journal of Risk and Insurance. (Q). Oriando. Department of Finance. College of Business University of Central Florida.

Journal of Small Business Management. (4/Yr). Wichita, KS. College of Business Administration, Wichita State University.

MSU Business Topics. (Q). Michigan State University, Michigan.

Management and Labour Studies. (Q). Jamshedpur. Xavier Labour Relations Institute.

Quarterly Review of Economics and business. (Q.) Champaign, IL. University of Illnois.

Review of Business and Economic Research. (Semi-Annual). New Orleans, LA. College of Business Administration, University of New Orleans.

Sloan Management Review. (3/Yr). Sloan School of Management, Massachusetts Institute of Technology, Cambridge, MA.

Vikalpa; the Journal for Decision Makers. (Q). 1976- Ahmedabad, Indian Institute of Management.

LIST OF JOURNALS HAVING ACADEMIC AND RESEARCH-BASED ARTICLES, DOCTORAL DISSERTATIONS AND RESEARCH IN PROGRESS

AGRICULTURE

Agri-business
Agricultural Economics
Agricultural Economics Research Review
Agricultural Situation in India
Agricultural Systems
American Economic Review
American Journal of Agricultural Economics
Austrian Journal of Agricultural Economics
Canadian Journal of Agricultural Economics
Economic and Political Weekly
Economic Journal
European Review of Agricultural Economics
Indian Journal of Agricultural Economics
International Journal of Water Resources Development
Journal of Agricultural Economics
Journal of Agricultural Engineering
Journal of Agricultural Engineering Research
Journal of Rural Development
Journal of Rural Studies
Land Economics

Oxford Agrarian Studies

Rural Sociology

Water Resources Bulletin

Water Resources Research

COMPUTER AND INFORMATION SYSTEMS

acm Transactions and Information Systems

Computers and Information Systems

Computers and Operations Research

Computers in Human Behaviour

Computers in Industry

Computer Surveys

Data Communications

Data Management

Datamation

IEEE Transactions on Computers

Information and Management Systems

Information and Software Technology

Information Processing and Management

Information Technology for Development

Journal of Computer and System Sciences

Journal of Information Systems Management

Journal of Systems Management

Software Practice and Experience

ECONOMICS

American Economic Review

American Journal of Agricultural Economics

Anvesak

Applied Economics

Asian Development Review

Business Horizons

Developing Economies
Econometrica
Economic and Political Weekly
Economic Development and Cultural Change
Economic Journal
Economica
Economics of Planning
Indian Economic Journal
Indian Economic Research
Indian Journal of Economics
Journal of Business
Journal of Common Market Studies
Journal of Economic History
Journal of Economic Literature
Journal of Economic Theory
Journal of Economics and business
Journal of Forecasting
Journal of Housing Economics
Journal of International Economics
Journal of Industrial Economics
Journal of International Development
Journal of Political Economy
Land Economics
Margin
National Institute Economic Review
Oxford Bulletin of Economics and Statistics
Oxford Economic Papers
Progress in Planning
Quarterly Journal of Economics
Quarterly Review of Economics and Business
Regional Science and Urban Economics

Review of Business and Economic Research
World Bank Economic Review
World Development
World Economy

FINANCE & ACCOUNTING

Abacus
Accountancy
Accounting & Business Research
Accounting, Organizations & Society
Accounting Review
American Economic Review
Applied Financial Economics
Business Horizons
California Management Review
Economic Journal
Finance India
Financial Analysis Journal
Financial Executive
Financial Management
Financial Review
Harward Business Review
Journal of Accountancy
Journal of Accountanting and Economics
Journal of Accounting and Public Policy
Journal of Accounting, Auditing & Finance
Journal of Accounting Literature
Journal of Accounting Research
Journal of business
Journal of Business Finance
Journal of Business Finance & Accounting

Journal of Common Market Studies

Journal of Finance

Journal of Financial & Quantitative Analysis

Journal of Financial Economics

Journal of Financial Management & Analysis

Journal of Financial Research

Journal of Foreign Exchange, & International Finance

Journal of International Financial Management & Accounting

Journal of Money, Credit & Banking

Journal of Portfolio Management

Review of Quantitative Finance & Accounting

Sloan Management Review

MANAGEMENT (BUSINESS POLICY)

ASCI Journal of Management

Academy of Management Journal

Academy of Management Review

Administrative Science Quarterly

Advanced Management Journal

Asian Entrepreneur

Business and Society

Business Horizons

British Journal of Management

Business Quarterly

Business Topics

Columbia Journal of World Business

Decision

Executive

Economic and Political Weekly

Journal of Business

iimb Review

Indian Journal of Public Enterprises

Indian Management

International Executive

International Management

Journal of Applied Management

Journal of Business

Journal of Business Research

Journal of Business Studies

Journal of Enterprise Management

Journal of Economics & Business

Journal of General Management

Journal of International Business Studies

Journal of Management Studies

Journal of Small Business Management

Journal of Business Strategy

Journal of the Institute of Public Enterprises

Management Decision

Management International Review

Management Review

Management Science

Managerial Planning

Multinational Business

Omega

Optimum; the Journal of Public Sector Management

Organizational Dynamics

Policy Sciences

Policy Studies Journal

Sloan Management Review

Strategic Management Journal

Vikalpa

MARKETING

American Economic Review
Business Horizons
California Management Review
European Journal of Marketing
Harward Business Review
Industrial Marketing
Industrial Marketing Management
International Journal of Advertising
International Journal of Research in Marketing
International Marketing Review
Journal of Advertising
Journal of Advertising Research
Journal of Business
Journal of Consumer Research
Journal of International Marketing & Marketing Research
Journal of Macro-marketing
Journal of Marketing
Journal of Marketing Research
Journal of Retailing
Journal of the Market Research Society
Marketing Communications
Marketing Letters
Marketing Research
Marketing Science
Operations Research Quarterly
Psychology and Marketing
Retail and Distribution Management

ORGANIZATIONAL BEHAVIOUR

Academy of Management Journal

Administrative Science Quarterly

American Journal of Sociology

American Sociological Review

British Journal of Sociology

Communication Research

Creativity Research Journal

Human Relations

Human Resource Management

Human Resource Management Review

Indian Journal of Psychology

Indian Journal of Social Science

Industrial Journal of Psychology

International Journal of Contemporary Sociology

International Journal of Organizational Analysis

Journal of Applied Behavioral Science

Journal of Behavioral Decision Making

Journal of Communication

Journal of Creative Behaviour

Journal of Enterprise Management

Journal of Experimental Social Psychology

Journal of Management Studies

Journal of Organizational Behaviour

Journal of Social Policy

Organizational Behaviour and Human Performance

Organizational Dynamics

Organizaiton Studies

Personnel Psychology

Social Research

Social Science Research

Sociological Methods and Research

PERSONNEL AND INDUSTRIAL RELATIONS

British Journal of Industrial Relations
Human Resource Planning
Indian Journal of Industrial Relations
Indian Journal of Labour Economics
Industrial and Labour Relations Review
Industrial Relations
Industrial Relations Journal
International Labour Review
Journal of Labour Economics
Journal of Labour Research
Journal of Managerial Psychology
Labour and Society
Management and Labour Studies
Personnel
Personnel Journal
Personnel Management
Personnel Psychology
Personnel Review

PRODUCTION AND QUANTITATIVE METHODS

American Journal of Mathematical and Management Sciences
Applied Statistics
Biometrica
Decision Sciences
Econometrica
Interfaces
International Journal of Management & Systems
International Journal of Operations & Production Management
International Journal of Production Economics
International Journal of Production Management

International Journal of Production Research
Journal of Applied Probabilities
Journal of Engineering & Technology Management
Journal of Management Studies
Journal of Operations Management
Journal of Policy Modeling
Journal of Product Innovation Management
Journal of Regional Sciences
Journal of the American Statistical Association
Journal of the Operations Research Society
Journal of Purchasing & Materials Management
Management Science
Mathematics of Operations Research
Naval Research Logistic Quarterly
Omega
Operations Research
Operations Research Letters
Operations Research Quarterly
Production & Inventory Management Journals
Production Planning and Control
Productivity
R & D Management
Research Management
Research Policy
SIAM Review
Technology Studies

PUBLIC SYSTEMS

Development Policy Review
Energy
Energy Economics

Energy Management
Energy Policy
Health Care Management Review
Health Policy and Planning
Indian Journal of Public Administration
Journal of communications
Journal of Development Economics
Journal of Health and Social Review
Journal of Human Resources
Journal of Public Economics
Journal of Policy Analysis and Management
Journal of Regional Science
Journal of Transport
Local Government Studies
Pacific and Asian Journalof Energy
Policy Sciences
Population Research and Policy Review
Public Administration
Public Administration and Development
Public Administration Review
Regional Development Dialogue
Review of Regional Studies
Transportation
Transportation Research
Transportation Science
Water Resources Bulletin
Water Resources Research
World Development

RESEARCH REPORTS/MONOGRAPHS

The research report/monograph is an account of research work done on a particular subject/project. It is usually a form of communication among scholars in a particular field. The results of research may be communicated in many forms like monographs/journals articles/conference papers. Academic and Research Institutes, or Organizations sponsored or supports the research project, and the researcher has to submit its upto date progress frequently. They have an advantage over journal articles as it is quickly published and disseminate the information to the interested in the same field. Journal article normally deal with the work which is completed whereas the reports can be used to find out the research in progress, and also gives the full details of the work done at each stage on a particular subject. The research monograph usually has been a very scholarly treatment of some aspect of theory written by a single author. The results of such research report may be read in the professional conference or may be issued as journal article or working paper.

STATISTICAL SOURCES

GOVERNMENT AND INTERNATIONAL AGENCIES

"The Government of a country is now tending to become the most prolific author and the biggest publisher in the country" rightly said by Dr. S.R. Ranganathan. Almost all countries of the world governments are the major compiler, analyser and the publishers of national statistics. Inter-governmental and international agencies like UN, UNESCO, ILO, WHO, UNDP, FAO, World Bank, OECD and others play the same role in compilation of international statistical data. The statistical data on various aspects are also being published by publications agencies, chambers of commerce, trade associations, professional bodies, banks, research associations and individual companies, to meet the needs of a set of readers.

In India, the Central as well as State Governments through its various ministries, departments, directorates, agencies, organizations, offices and other bodies published literature on a wide variety of subjects. These publications are reliable, up-to-date and inexpensive source of information on practically every subject of current interest and topics. Their importance as primary sources of research is beyond doubt. They are not merely dry statistical records, but provides all trends of human activites. They are the living records useful to general public, researchers, scholars, academicians, business executives and policy makers.

Now, in the fast developing and complex society, all aspects of business planning whether it is purchasing, production, labour, marketing, finance, investment or general policy necessiate an increasing use of statistics.

The need for more and better forecasting largely dependent on statistics. Statistical information can be important for many business purposes, investment decisions, market research, comparisons of costs, whether of labour, machinery or production, monitoring trends in prices, wages, unemployment etc., and changes in population and household composition. Published statistics do not provide tailor-made answers to a particular problem but they may help in finding solutions both in broad strategic planning and in day-to-day decision making. It is always worth checking published data before embarking on one's own data collection or research.

The most useful data to management experts, business executives and researchers is derived from government departments, and its many agencies, like Central Statistical Organization, Labour Bureau, National Sample Survey Organisation (NSSQ) Directorate General and Various Activities, Bureau of Public Enterprises, Department of Company Affairs, Labour Bureau Department of Industrial Development, Director General of Technical Development (DGTD), Development commissioners, RBI, Ofices of the various Commissions, Registrar General of Census Operations, Planning Commission, Cabinet Secretariat etc. etc. They need various types of statistical data on economic and social; demography, housing, science and technology, labour, energy, education, agriculture, employment, irrigation, rural development, industry, trade, production, export and import, prices, financial, planning and so on. The most convenient way to start a statistical search for the above subjects is to refer the statistical abstracts and other statistical handbooks published by various State and Central Government Agencies. The data on the topics mentioned above can be available in any business schools library reference section. The Central Statistical Organisation has published the following guide which describes in detail the latest sources published by the government publishing agencies.

Guide to official statistics. 3rd edition, India. Central Statistical Organisation, Ministry of Planning, 1987. The scope of the guide is given below for easy reference of the publication.

The guide is divided in 3 parts covering 16 chapters dealing with "Social Statistics", 'Economic Statistics' and 'Other Statistics'. It helps the users of official data in identifying the relevant sources of particular data, methodology used for collection of data and interpretation of the statistical series available in official publication, and attempts to make available on up-to-date information regarding the statistics released in the 'recurrent publications of those organisation'. A publication index containing the list of the publications referred to in the guide is given.

There are many publications having the statistical data but below are some of the very standard publications.

SOME STATISTICAL PUBLICATIONS- GOVERNMENT

1. Agricultural Prices in India. 1987-88.
2. Agricultural Wages in India. 1989-90.
3. Cooperative Movement in India; A Statistical Profile, 1989.
4. Annual Survey of Industries 1983-84 (Factory Sector) 15 v. Calcutta, C.S.O. 1989 and Summary results for factory sector for the year 1987-88 separately available.
5. Area and Production of Principal Crops in India: 1988-89, India. Directorate of Economics and Statistics, 1990.
6. Basic Statistics to Indian economy - 1989. India. C.S.O. 1989.
7. Basic Statistics Relating to Indian Economy. 1950-51 to 1988-89. India, C.S.O., 1989. Bulletin on Food Statistics, 1989. India. Directorate of Economic and Statistics.
8. Directory of Joint Stock Companies in India. 8 Vols. India. Department of Company Affairs, 1991.
9. Estimates of State Domestic Product and Gross Fixed Capital Formation, 1991. India, C.S.O.
10. 1982-83 Handbook of Housing Statistics.
11. Handbook of Industrial Statistics 1989. India. ministry of Industry, Delhi, Controller of Publications, 1989.
12. Indian Agriculture Statistics 1981-82 to 1985-86.
13. Indian Annual Coal Statistics, 1987.
14. Indian Fertilizers Statistics, 1990-91.
15. Indian Forest Statistics, 1973.

16. Indian Livestock Census, V. 1, 1982.
17. Monthly Statistical Abstract of India.
18. Monthly Statitics of Foreign Trade of India 2Vo]s.
19. National Accounts Statistics, 1988-89. New Delhi, C.S.O.
20. Statistical Abstracts of India, 1989. New Delhi, C.S.O., 1990.
21. State Statistical Abstracts. (Statistical Abstracts are also published by all States and of Districts also).
22. Statistics of the Foreign Trade of India, 1980.
23. Statistical Pocket Book. India, 1990. New Delhi, C.S.O., 1990.
24. Indian Labour Yearbook 1988 (Labour Bureau)
25. Labour Bureau's Labour 1989
26. Pocketbook of Labour Statistics 1990 (Labour Bureau)
27 Statistical Profile on Women Labour 1986 (Labour Bureau)

SOME STATISTICAL PUBLICATIONS-INTERNATIONAL ORGANIZATIONS AND AGENCIES

Handbook of International Trade and Development Statistics - 1990. New York, United Nations, 1991.

Industrial Statistics Yearbook - 1988. 2v. N.Y. UNO, 1990.

International Financial Statistics Yearbook 1985. Washington, IMF.

International Trade Statistics Yearbook - 1989. New York. United Nations, 1991.

Latest Information on National Accounts of Developing Countries available end December 1990. Paris, OECD, 1991.

Production Yearbook - 1989. Rome. Food and Agricultural Organization of the United Nations.

Social Indicaters of Development, 1990. Washington, World Bank.

Statistical Yearbook - 1987. New York, United Nations, 1988.

Statistical Yearbook - 1991. Paris, UNESCO.

Statistical Yearbook for Asia and the Pacific 1989. Thailand, ESCAP, 1989.1989.

Trends in Developing Economies, 1991. Washington, World Bank, 1991. World Debt Tables: 1991-92. Washington, World Bank, 1991.

World Economic Survey - 1991. New York, United Nations, 1991

World Energy Statistics, 1985. N.Y. UNO.

World Resources: 1990-91; New York, UNEP, 1990-91.

World Tables: 1989-90. Washington, IBRD, 1989-90

Yearbook of Labour Statistics - 1991. Geneva, ILO, 1991.

Yearbook of National Accounts Statistics - 1987. N.Y., United Nations, 1988.

World Development Report 1992.

STATISTICAL PUBLICATIONS - NON-GOVERNMENT

All aspects of business planning whether they may be production, purchasing, labour, marketing, finance, investments or general policy have necessitated an increasing use of statistics. From past and present statistical trends future events can be expected to be discussed and correct decisions are made more easily. The need for more and better forecasting depends on statistics. Important statistical compilations are also produced by non-government bodies; private agencies; chambers of commerce, trade associations, research institutes and organizations and companies, both national and international. It must be noted that some important statistics are found in trade journals, directories and yearbooks, and also in the annual reports. The following are some of the many statistical publications available.

Almost every country in the world collects, samples, analyses and publishes more or less the same kind of statistical data in more or less the same amount of detail.

SOME STATISTICAL PUBLICATIONS-NON-GOVERNMENT

Agricultural Statistical Compendium. *2 pts. New Delhi. Techno-Economic Research Institute.*

Annual Sales Statistics: 1989-90. *Calcutta. Steel Authority of India.*

Banking Statistics 1985

Centre for Monitoring Indian Economy. *Economic htelligence* Service. Bombay.

The authoritative, upto date and exhaustive data statistics listed in the following category: 1. World context. 2. Macro Framework of the Indian Economy. 3. Current Economic Situation and Progress- a) Monthly Review of Indian Economy b) Index Numbers of Wholesale Prices; Weekly Data c) Others. 4. Energy and Natural Resources. 5. Agricultural Sector. 6. Industrial Sector. 7. Forms on Industrial Units and Projects. 8. Economic Indicators: Folders. Under each category mentioned above the CMIE publishes various publications.

Fertilizer Statistics: 1990-91. New Delhi, Fertilizer Association of India.

Finances of Large Public Limited Companies 1987-88

Handbook of Statistics - 1989. New Delhi, Confederation of Engineering Industry, 1990.

India Database; The Economy: Annual Time Series Data, by H.L. Chandhok and The Policy Group. 2v. New Delhi. Living Media India Ltd., 1990.

The author has done a remarkable work by putting together a comprehensive data base on the Indian economy - and have bridged an important gap in the road to improve applied econometric work in India. Moreover, economists will now find work on macro-econometric models for policy simulation simpler since all the data in these two volumes have been systematically collected and presented in a form that is easily accessible. The author has saved students, academics, journalists and policy makers innumerable man-hours of research work, Vol. 1 includes the data on: 'National Accounts'; 'Prices' and 'Public Finance', whereas the Vol. 2 has data on 'Agriculture', 'Money, Banking, Currency and Coinage', 'Foreign Trade and Balance of Payments' and 'Industry'. The data given is from pre-plan 1950-51 to seventh plan i.e. 1987-88. This computerised large data bank occupies 21 floppy disks.

India - Economic Information Yearbook: 1991-92, by A.N. Agrawal, and others. New Delhi, National Publishing House, 1992.

Industrial Databook: 1991-92. New Delhi. Centre for Industrial and Economic Research.

Information India 1990-91 Global View by S.P. Agrawal and J.C. Aggarwal. New Delhi, Concept Publishing co., 1992.
This is the most comprehensive industrial integrated data system, logging over 20,000 data entries.

Kothari's Industrial Directory of India: 1992. Madras, Kothari Enterprises, 1992.
This is a valuable encyclopaedia on the Indian Corporate Sector, carries financial analysis of over 2500 Joint Stock Components spread through the sub-continent.

Kothari's Yearbook on Business and Industry - 1990. Madras, Kothari & Kothari, 1990.
The Publication starts with an Economic Survey, provides certain vital data on each of the public limited companies arranged industrywise.

Operational Statistics 1990-91. New Delhi, Industrial Finance Corporation of India

Report on Development banking in India 1990-91. Bombay, Industrial Development Bank of India.

Report on Currency and Finance 1990-91

Statistics for Iron and Steel Industry in India: 1990. New Delhi, Steel Authority of India.

Statistical Outline of India: 1989-90. Bombay, Tata Services Ltd., 1989.

Stock Exchange Official Directory. 18 Vols. Bombay. Bombay Stock Exchange.
This is a loose-leaf directory, continuously kept up-to-date.

CENSUS - 1981

Just as the Indian Census has over the hundred and more years of its existence been more than a mere head count, its publications too have gone for beyond the prescribed presentation of information collected in the course of the Census operations. This has resulted in a large output of multi-disciplinary literature lying in various areas of enquiry and expertise and exploring and righting up several facts of people and their lives in all corners of this great country. These publications have been emanating variously from special studies, collaborative research, workshops and seminars, plan schemes and so on.

The Indian Census remains the primary source of national population data for administration and for many aspects of economic and social planning. The first census was taken between 1865 and 1872, the next was in 1881 and thereafter every ten years without a break. The latest census taken in 1981 covers twenty-three states, nine union territories and 572 districts. The 1981 census publications consists of 32 series - Series I represents all Indian tables and reports; series 2 to 32 covers the census of each state and the union territory.

The following is the scheme of the 1981 Census of India Publications:

I. Regular Publications:

Series 1 India

States:

Series 2 Andhra Pradesh

Series 3 Assam

Series 4 Bihar

Series 5 Gujarat

Series 6 Haryana

Series 7 Himachal Pradesh

Series 8 Jammu & Kashmir

Series 9 Karnataka

Series 10 Kerala

Series 11 Madhya Pradesh

Series 12 Maharashtra

Series 13 Manipur

Series 14 Meghalaya

Series 15 Nagaland

Series 16 Orissa

Series 17 Punjab

Series 18 Rajasthan

Series 19 Sikkim

Series 2- Tamil Nadu

Series 21 Tripura

Series 22 Uttar Pradesh

Series 23 West Bengal

Union Territories:

Series 24 Andaman & Nicobar Islands

Series 25 Arunachal Pradesh

Series 26 Chandigarh.

Series 27 Dadra & Nagar Haveli

Series 28 Delhi

Series 29 Goa, Daman & Diu

Series 30 Lakshadweep

Series 31 Mizoram

Series 32 Pondicherry

For all Indian and for each state and Union Territory the 1981 census tables/reports are broadly published according to the plan given below.

Part I - A Administrative Report - Enumeration

Part I - B	Administrative Report - Tabulation (For official use only)
Part II - A	General Population Tables
Part II - B	Primary Census Abstract
Part III	General Economic Tables
Part IV	Social and Cultural Tables
Part V	Migration Tables
Part IV	Fertility Tables
Part VII	Houses and Disabled Population
Part VIII	Household tables
Part IX	Special Tables on Scheduled Castes & Scheduled Tribes
Part X(A)	Town Directory
Part X(B)	Survey Reports on Selected Towns
Part X(C)	Survey Reports on Selected Villages
Part XI	Ethnographic notes and special studies on Scheduled Castes and Scheduled Tribes
Part XII	Census Atlas
Part XIII	District Census Handbooks

II. Census papers, Occasional papers, Monographs etc.

CENSUS - 1991

The Indian Census has not been a mere statistical operation, Demographic data have been interpreated and analysed in an interesting and revealing manner. A large number of experts have been associated with the census and their analysis of data has often been the only authentic material on socio-economic conditions. The socio-economic surveys of hundreds of villages will indeed be useful for research workers in economics, sociology and interdisciplinary subjects. It is by far the most important single source of socio-economic data in the country.

The Registrar General & Census Commissioner of India have published the provisional population tables of 1991 census for India as well as the States. Subsequently, the various Directors of census operations for the states and Union Territories rushed up their results individually and also for the districts concerned. Based on the first results of the census 1991, the Economic Intelligence Service of Centre for Monitoring Indian Economy, Bombay, have brought out the document entitled "1991 Census" - First Results (For All-India, States & Districts) in respect of information available on population, sex ratio, density of population, growth rate of population, literary rates at all- India, State and district levels and urban centres each having population of one lakh and above alongwith male/female population, sex ratio and literary levels, properly processed and presented.

Recently, the Registrar General and Census Commissioner have published two papers on "Provisional Population Tables - 1991" and some more provisional volumes and occassional papers are also published by Director of Census Operations.

The Publication series is as follows:-

1. India.

STATES

2. Andhra Pradesh
3. Assam
4. Arunachal Pradesh
5. Bihar
6. Goa
7. Gujarat
8. Haryana
9. Himachal Pradesh
10. Jammu & Kashmir
11. Karnataka
12. Kerala
13. Madhya Pradesh
14. Maharashtra
15. Manipur
16. Meghalaya
17. Mizoram
18. Nagaland
19. Orissa
20. Punjab
21. Rajasthan
22. Sikkim
23. Tamil Nadu
24. Tripura
25. Uttar Pradesh
26. West Bengal

UNION TERRITORIES

27. Andman & Nicobar Island
28. Chandigarh
29. Dadra & Nagar Haveli
30. Delhi

31. Daman & Diu

32. Lakshadweep

33. Pondicherry

For all-India and for each State and Union Territory, the census tabulations and reports will be published according to the following plan:

Part I-	Administration Report (for official use only)
Part II-	General Population Tables
Part III-	General Economic Tables
Part IV-	Social and Cultural Tables
Part V-	Migration Tables
Part VI-	Fertility Tables
Part VII-	Tables on Houses and Household Amenities
Part VIII-	Special Tables on Scheduled Castes and Scheduled Tribes
Part IX-	Town Directory,, Survey Report on Town and Villages
Part X	
Part XI-	Census Atlas
Part XII-	District Census Handbook

The following special papers are also planned and will be published as and when they are ready as 1991 Census Papers:

(a) Special studies taken up by the Directors of Census Operations

(b) Special Areas Surveys.

(c) Special Tables for Standard Urban Area

(d) Language Survey Reports

(e) Post Enumeration Check Report.

(f) Age Tables.

(g) LifeTables.

(h) Reports on estimates of inter - censal birth and death rates using 1981-91 Life Tables and age data.

(i) Development of Vital Statistics in India

Besides these special papers, some monographs based on 1991 Census data on subjects of topical interest to be prepared by scholars will be brought out as 1991 Census Monographs.

It is also proposed to carry out some special Studies of 1991 Census data in Collaboration with other organisations and the results of such studies will be published as occasional Papers of the 1991 Census.

It is also proposed to disseminate census tabulations and the basic data in machine readable forms such as maganetic tapes, diskkettes, floppies etc.

CURRENT AWARENESS SERVICE/CURRENT CONTENTS

It is not possible for even the most avid reader to keep up to date with regular reading in his specific area because of the increased flow of publications and periodicals in the world. There is always a time lag between the publication of an article in a journal and its reference in abstracting and indexing journal. To cater to the needs of teachers, researchers and doctoral students, many individual academic and research libraries have started keeping control on the information explosion by providing current awareness services. Some libraries provide a list of new books, and the articles from the recently received journals in the library in mimeograph form to be circulated within the institute or the organisation. Some libraries provide their own services by photocopying the contents pages of some selected journals in specific areas and circulate to the members working in that area. Obviously, the periodicals covered by the contents lists should be those which the users would like to refer to regularly. Before, this service is started it is essential to consult the faculty and researchers to find out their needs of periodicals which they wish to scan. In this way, the researcher can scan through the contents of various journals and select the articles of his interest. The purpose of CAS is to disseminate current information. They are primarily produced for domestic use in a particular institute or organization. Vikram Sarabhai Library of the Indian Institute of Management, Ahmedabad has started this service for internal use since last four years.

Some of the "Contents Pages Services" are as follows:

Contents of Recent Economics Journals (W) HMSO

Covers a wider field of economics covering 50 periodicals. It includes finance, taxation, agriculture, regional and business economics.

Contents Pages in Management (Fornightly). England, Manchester Business School Library.

It consists of contents pages of all the main management and business periodicals received in the Manchester Business School Library. It also lists of working papers generated in most of the leading business schools.

Computer Contents (Semi-M.) 1983-. Philadelphia, PA., Institute for Scientific Information.

A Compilation of tables of contents from more than 250 of the latest computer periodicals.

Current Contents: Social and Behavioral Sciences. (1969-) W. Philaddelphia, P.A. Institute for Scientific Information.

Tables of contents of the world's leading publications covering social and behavioral sciences.

Finance India (Q). Delhi, Indian Institute of Finance.

It gives the contents of some of the selected current periodicals publishing articles relating to Finance and Accounting.

International Current Awareness Service. (M) Comp. by British Library of Political and Economic Science at the London School of Economics. Routledge, London.

It is immediate, comprehensive and ease-to-use tool for accessing the latest in the world's constantly expanding social science literature. Its coverage is of the world's journal literature through a service that scans at least 120,000 articles in a year, on Economics, Sociology, Political Science and Anthropology.

Journal Contents in Quantitative Methods. (M) 1979- Univ. of Manchester, Institute of Science and Technology, School of Management Sciences Manchester, England.

Contains contents pages of Journals in Statistics and Operations Research and Quantitative Journals in the Management Sciences.

Journals of Economic Literature (Q) Nashville. Tenn. American Economic Association

The Journal contains the contents pages of a number of scholarly and research oriented journals in the field.

Long Range Planning (Bi-M.). New York, Pergamon Press

Each issue contains a 'Current Awareness Service' on the subject 'Long Range Planning'.

Management Contents. (Semi-M.). Management Contents, Cartson Drive, Suite 500, Northbook Il 60062, USA.

Contents reproduces the contents pages from a selection of about 350 business and management periodicals.

SELECTIVE DISSEMINATION OF INFORMATION : (SDI)

Selective dissemination of information is a personalised service, providing individuals or groups of individuals working together with references to newly published information on the topic or topics in which they are interested. Library staff may produce a alert bulletin which is circulated to members which outlines the new literature, divided into subject areas which reflect the subject interests of these members. With the current awareness bulletin, the user himself selects the items in which he is interested from the many items listed in each issue, where SDI services the selection process is performed by matching the user profile. One of the main advantages of SDI is that the profile can be tailored to suit the exact requirements of the individual user. Individual members make a formal list of their professional subject interest. Each list is translated into a user profiles. This is a service that can be provided with a manual system but if this services is to be really effective and efficient an automated system is necessary. Greater sophistication usually depends on the library using a computer. These profiles are feed into the computer and matched with the profiles for new acquisitions which have been put together. In this way the members are informed at regular interval of any new literature which match their interests. This service is very useful to the Faculty and Research Community. Some method of feedback is essential with this type of service to ensure that the user is receiving the information he needs.

WORKING PAPERS

Working papers are considred as useful research literature on management. They are known as research reports, dicsussion papers, seminar papers, research study etc. Business schools, academic and research councils or university departments produce working papers to be circulated among their own organizations or to selected institutions and individuals. They provide the first available draft of a proposed publication, and they are drafts of potential journal articles or for the papers to be submitted to seminars and conferences. They are being circulated or kept in the library to be referred by the interested area people to comment before submitting the final draft to a journal or seminar for publication. To get the working papers of other institutions, the researcher should contact where similar type of research is being conducted. The papers are mostly in the memeographed forms and being in a limited circulation.

Some of the Indian and Foreign Institutes which publish "Working Papers" are listed below:

IIM, Ahmedabad

IIM, Calcutta

NIBM, Poona. (National Institute of Bank Management)

IRMA, Anand. (Institute for Rural Management)

Centre for Development Studies, Trivandrum

GIAP, Ahmedabad. (Gujarat Institute of Area Planning)

IPE, Hyderabad. (Institute of Public Enterprises)

WB. World Bank

OECD. Organization for Economic Cooperation and Development

UNCRD. United Nationsl Centre for Regional Development Nagoya, Japan.

ISNAR. International Service for National Agricultural Research, Netherlands

NBER. National Bureau of Economic Research, New York

IBRD, Washington. International Bank for Reconstruction and Development

Delhi School of Economics. University of Delhi

University of California. Berkerly Business School.

NCAER, New Delhi. National Council of Applied Economic Research

The following are some of the sources:

Abstracts of Working Papers in Economics (Q). 1983-. England, Cambridge University Press.

Contents Pages in management (W). Manchester, Manchester Business School Library

It includes all the working papers, published by leading business schools.

Current Management Research: Index and Abstracts of Working Papers (Annual) 1982-. Trans-Media-Univ. of Warmick.

The publication lists working papers published all over the world arranged by author, institutions and subject.

University Research in Business and Economics, A Bibliography (Annual). Association of University Business and Economic Research.

It lists working papers by subject and institutions having an author index.

REVIEWS

Reviews are the important sources for any researcher as they represent the state of the art in a given subject. It starts with some historical introduction with an assessment of the current status of the subject including most recent development, covered new ideas, some controversies and future directions. An exhaustive bibliography is published in the reviews and serves as an additional source for the most recent literature on the subject. A few reviews in a serial form published annually and starting with the titles like:

1. Advances in .....
2. Annual review of/in.....
3. Progress in.....
4. Research in......
5. Survey of Research in.....

A few examples of the "Research Annuals" are:

1. Advances in Accounting	v.1-; 1984-
Advances in Accounting Information System	v.1-; 1986-
Advances in Applied Business Strategy	v.1-; 1984-
Advances in Applied Social Psychology	v.1-; 1984-) (Irregular)
Advances in Arithamatical Programming and Financial Planning	v.1-; 1986-
Advances in Business Marketing	v.1-; 1986-
Advances in Computer Programming Management	(Irregular)
Advances in Computer Research	v.1-; 1983-
Advances in Consumer Research	v.1-; 1974-
(Pros. Brigham Univ. Graduate Schools of Mana.)	
Advances in Financial Planning & Forecasting	v.1-; 1985-
Advances in Industrial and Labour Relations	v.1-; 1983-
Advances in International Marketing	v.1-; 1987-

	Title	Coverage
	Advances in Organizational Development (W.J. Ablex Pub. corp.)	v.1-; 1989-
	Advances in Psychology	v.47-; 1987- (Irregular)
	Advances in Strategic Management	v.1-; 1983-
	Advanced Series in Management (Netherlands, Elsevier Science Pub.)	v.12-; 1988- (Irregular)
2.	Annual Review of Information Science and Technology N.Y. Interscience	v.12-; 1966-77
	Annual Review in Automatic Programming Oxford, Pergamon Press	v.1-; 1960- (Annual)
3.	Progress in Experimental Personality Research (N.Y. Academic Press)	v.1-; 1964-
	Progress in Marketing (England Printer Pub. Ltd.)	1989-
	Progress in Operations Research (N.Y. John Wiley)	v.1-; 1961-
	Progress in Resource Management and Environmental Planning (N.Y. John Wiley)	v.1-; 1979-
4.	Research in Consumer Behaviour	v.1-; 1985-
	Research in Corporate Social Performance and Policy	v.1-; 1978-
	Research in Domestic and International Agri-Business Management	v.1-; 1980-
	Research in Economic History	v.1-; 1976-
	Research in Experimental Economics	v.1-; 1979-
	Research in Finance	v.1-; 1979-
	Research in Human Capital & Development	v.1-; 1979-
	Research in International business & Finance	v.1-; 1977-
	Research in Labor Economics	v.1-; 1977-
	Research in Marketing	v.1-; 1986-
	Research in Organizational Behaviour	v.1-; 1979-
	Research in Organizational Change and Development	v.1-; 1987 -

Research in Personnel and Human Resource Management v.1-; 1983-

Research in Political Economy v.1-; 1978-

Research in Public Policy Analysis and Management v.1-; 1975-

Research in Public Sector Economics v.1-; 1986-

Research in Rural Sociology & Development v.1-; 1984-

Research in Technological Innovation, Management and Policy v.1-; 1983-

Research in the Sociology of Organizations v.1-; 1982-

Research in the Sociology of Work v.1-; 1982-

Research in Transportation Economics v.1-; 1983-

5. Survey of Research in Economics and Social History of India.

New Delhi, ICSSR, 1986

Survey of Research in Economics, 7v. 1975- New Delhi, ICSSR Bombay (1st and 2nd Survey)

Research in Economics (2nd Survey)

Survey of Research in Management (2nd Survey) ed. by B.L. Maheshwari

Research in Management - 1970-79 (2nd Survey) New Delhi, ICSSR

Survey of Research in Psychology. 2v. 1973. New Delhi, ICSSR, Bombay (1st, 2nd, 3rd Survey)

Survey of Research in Sociology and Social Anthropology. 3v. 1972. New Delhi, ICSSR, Bombay, Popular (1st & 2nd Series)

There are other important ICSSR Surveys of Research:

Accounting Theory

Demography

Political Science

Public Administration, 2nd series (1970-79)

The "Research Annuals" listed at No. 1 and 3 are published by, Jay Press Inc., Connecticut, and London. They represent a diverse set of papers that represent current research in the field.

CHAMBERS OF COMMERCE AND INDUSTRY

There are regional, national and international chambers of commerce and industry, concerned with every aspect of industrial production; commercial developments and governmental relations and civic affairs. They serve as a central agency for individuals, firms, companies and trade associations for promoting and protecting business interest. The functions are to provide services to its members primarily through the provisions of information on such matters as legislation, taxation, trading conditions at home and abroad, conditions affecting imports and exports, procedure regarding controls, tariff, customs regulations and similar other topics. A few chambers of commerce have set up their own research division for carrying on economic research to encourage scientific research on all economic problems and to provide facilities and to arrange for training in practical business management. Many chambers of commerce to name a few like Indian Merchants Chambers, Bombay; Federation of Indian Chambers of Commerce and Industry, Punjab, Haryana & Delhi Chambers of Commerce and Industry, Associated chamber of commerce and industry of India, (all in New Delhi) have uptodate library and documentation services. Their libraries have good collection of books; trade journals; directories; areas reference books; commercial guides and press cuttings; survey reports and information about the existing and the newly established companies; tariffs; export/import regulations; government policy and notifications; and names of business contracts. Advance research scholars, workers, and doctoral students from different universities and institutions are making use of their library facilities. These chambers of commerce are publishing journals and books regarding the economic aspects of the country, government policies and on many other subjects relating to business and industry. From time to time special studies are also conducted by them on requests from members. Researchers can avail the facilities of their libraries by contacting the librarian in advance.

CORPORATION PUBLICATIONS/ANNUAL REPORTS

Company's own publications are the best sources of information about a company's activities and operations. A clear picture of any company can be obtained from its own published reports - i.e. Annual Reports. These publications provide information on the company, its product, and its future expansion in business.

The basic reporting document being Annual Reports, discharge a wealth of information about a company's performance, plans and products and sometimes include statistical information and projects the image of the company. From time to time or at some memorable occasions company publishes the documents describing its history, growth, and various aspects of their operations. These documents project a very valuable aspects of their companies and future activities, among its shareholders and potential shareholders.

Company's house journals are also a source of information. Although it has a limited circulation among the members only, it contains certain information on research and other activities and also some product information; general interest articles; social news and information about employees.

TRADE ASSOCIATIONS

Trade Associations may be local, regional or national.Trade Associations are established for coming together to advance the common economic interest and to gather data for its members. These associations are a valuable sources for the information on the developments of a particular industry or product; its structure and its statistics. Their basic purpose is to assist members and their industries in dealing with common business problems in several areas like: commercial and industrial research, standardization, statistics, trade promotions and relations with the government, labour and the general public. They publish statistical information, the progress about a industry, government policy and their representation to the government about their problems etc., in their annual publications or in their monthly or quarterly journals. The information is generally meant for their members, but non-members can also make use of it for a specific purpose.

CONFERENCE/SEMINAR PROCEEDINGS

The sponsoring institute/organisation publishes the proceedings of the conference in a volume before or after the conference/seminar. The papers presented are mostly the results of recently completed research or continuing work. Some papers at a conference are the fruit of recent research and are valuable in that they review current advances and provide information about them. The papers are most uptodate in the area. Many conference papers are similar in nature to journal articles; of particular interest are reviews, or state-of-the-art surveys, which feature at most conferences. Sometimes, the conference proceedings are not being published for years to come, but the quicker way to get the reprint is to approach/write to the author directly. Information about the fourthcoming conferences/seminars with names/the titles and authors are announced in the academic and professional journals.

Recent conference proceedings can give a good indication of the present position of work in a subject field, especially with regard to the various kinds of approach made by different workers. Some conferences are multi-disciplinary in character; the proceedings of these bring together ideas from people in different subject areas, and can stimulate new lines of enquiry.

Conference proceedings are published in its regular issues, or in a special supplement, or are published in a number of different journals. It is sometimes necessary to make direct contact with the author of a conference paper or organisation concerned, in order to get a copy of the paper.

ONLINE DATA BASES/SYSTEMS

One of the most recent means of searching current material is through on-line data bases. This method is very useful to the researcher as many of the databases focus more on journal articles. There are statistical databases also available, and in combination with textual databases provide a sufficiently large information base. Several online databases are available world wide covering a vast range of subjects. It is estimated that in 1984 there were more than 50 bibliographic data bases which specialized in business and management subjects and several other functional areas. On line information has provided a new dimension to information retrieval. The databases produced commercially are growing at a great pace and covering almost all specific and special disciplines of study and research.

Indian Council of Agricultural Research (ICAR) New Delhi

The ICAR established an Agricultural Research Information Centre at New Delhi to provide a Central Source of Information on the nature, location and status of current research projects conducted in the country in the field of agricultural sciences. The AGRIS-International /system for Agricultural Science and Technology based on the philosophy of the INIS, under the broad framework of UNISIST Programme, was established in 1974. It is essentially a mission oriented information system covering the entire field of agricultural science and technology. About 7000 Indian research projects have been listed involving nearly 30,000 research workers at the 42 ICAR research institutions/ laboratories, 26 agricultural universities etc. The major portion of the Indian input is in English. The ARIC has identified 100 core periodicals published in India and it scanes, selects and prepares the input to AGRIS according to the standard procedure.

Indian National Scientific Documentation Centre (INSDOC), New Delhi

The INSDOC is perhaps the first organization in India to use computer for information services such as union catalogue of scientific serials, roster of Indian translators, author/subject indexes for the Indian Science Abstracts, SDI service using the CAN/SDI software and databases like CA-Search, INSPEC and COMPENOEX, etc. Since 1981, a minicomputer system HP1000 series has been installed by NIC at INSDOC to work as a terminal to the mainframe system, CDC-Cyber-170 model 720. Recently, INSDOC has added a PSI-Circus-32 computer system and a Microvax system.

International Information System in Agricultural Science and Technology _ (AGRIS)

The main objective is to improve and expedite the exchange of agricultural information among nations of the world. It also aims at meeting the information needs of developing countries and help them to train their scientific and technical personnel also. It covers the entire field of agricultural science and technology. AGRIS formally started its operation of AGRINDEX from January 1975. Like INIS, AGRIS is a decentralised system in which each country is responsible for identifying records for documents published wihin its borders - AGRINDEX covers references on all branches of Agricultural Sciences, Plant sciences, Animal Sciences, Veterinary, Fisheries, Foods and Nutrition arranged under 85 subject categories alongwith author, commodities, geographic report and patent indexes. At the close of 1986, 122 countries were participating in AGRIS of which 117 were contributing inputs to AGRIS. In addition to this 14 multinational countries and FAO documentation centre and other international organizations are also contributing inputs.

International Nuclear Information System (INIS):

The main objective is to provide a comprehensive nuclear information announcement and abstracting service, using modern computer and micrographic techniques. It started functioning in April 1970. INIS Atominde was published in May 1970. INIS is an international system for the storage and retrieval of bibliogrpahic information and documents in the field of nuclear science and technology where sixty-seven member states of the IAEA and fourteen international organizations such as ISO, FAO, UNESCO, etc. are taking active part. The combined input exceeds 75,000 published items a year. The total number of items in the INIS bibliographic file was over 8 lakhs items in 1983. INIS works with full cooperation from the member states and further cooperation among its member states for mutual benefits of efforts in controlling the world's scientific literature in the field of nuclear science and technology with the object of achieving maximum economy in time, money, and effort and also to avoid duplication at various levels such as document generation, document processing, and document storage and dissemination.

ICMR-NIC-Centre for Bio-Medical Information, New Delhi

Medical literature Analysis Retieval System (MEDLARS) on-line (MEDLINE) is one of the world's largest medical database that is produced by the National Library of Medicine (USA). It is also one of the most used medical database covering approximately 3000 medical journals in 60 languages from all over the world. It contains over 2,00,000 references per year.

National Centre for Science Information (UGC-SIC) (NCSI) at Indian Institute of Science, Bangalore

The UGC funded the creation of NCSI for offering an up-to-date information service in individual subject areas to faculty, scientists, and research scholars. Since 1984, the centre is operating a large scale S.D.I. service covering the science disciplines. viz. PHYSICS, CHEMISTRY, BIOLOGY, MATHEMATICS and GEOLOGY. The primary objective of NCSI has been to give uptodate current awareness service to the research community in Indian Universities and colleges. Currently more than 10 lakhs bibliographic citations from five databases are annually processed to serve more than 3000 users.

National Information System for Science and Technology (NISSAT), New Delhi

NISSAT was established in 1977 with broad objectives of (a) information resource development, (b) identification of information users and (c) Manpower development. NISSAT has so far set up seven Sectoral Information Centres (SIC)to perform national level tasks in the areas mentioned below:

Name of the Sectoral Information Centre		Institution
i)	NICLAI (Leather Technology)	Central Leather Research Institute, Madras
ii)	NICFOS - (Food Science)	Central Food & Technological Research Institute, Mysore
iii)	NICMAP - (Machine Tools)	Central Machine Tools Research Institute, Bangalore
iv)	NICDAP - (Drugs and Pharmaceautical)	Central Drug Research Institute, Lucknow
v)	NICTAS (Textile and Allied Subjects)	Ahmedabad Textile Industry Research Association, Ahmedabad
vi)	NICHEM (Chemistry)	National Chemical Laboratory Pune
vii)	NICRYS (Crystallography)	Dept. of Crystallography University of Madras, Madras

National Medical Library (NML), New Delhi

The NML, under the Director General of Health Services, functions as a nodel agency for collection, processing and supply of biomedical information generated within the country and outside. It proposes to meet the requirements of biomedical community research workers, teachers, medical practitioners, administrators, planners and others concerned with health and its related disciplines. The NML conducts training courses in Health Science Librarianship. The Documentation Unit of NML provides:

i) Indexing and abstracting of health sciences literature published in India.

ii) Compilation of bibliographies

iii) Generating SDI and CAS

iv) Developing necessary tools like catalogues, manuals, guides, thesauri, directories etc.

National Social Science Documentation Centre (NASSDOC), New Delhi

The NASSDOC was set up in 1970 by ICSSR (Indian Council of Social Science Research) to build up a strong document collection particularly by collecting (a) published doctoral theses approved by Indian Universities and foreign theses in India, (b) research reports of the projects undertaken by ICSSR and other social science research institutions assisted by ICSSR (c) working papers presented at ICSSR funded seminars and conferences (d) periodicals of research in social sciences. The NASSDOC has created a strong documentary database of Ph.D. theses approved by Indian Universities. It provides input data regarding Indian publications to the International Committee for Social Sciences Information and Documentation, Paris; the International Bulletin of Bibliography on Education published from Madrid and the International Geographic Bibliography published from Paris.

The Popline (Population online)

Database created by Johns Hopkins and Columbia University Population Centres is at present located at the National Library of Medicine. The database gives information on sociological and biomedical aspects of population. The ICMR-NIC Centre provides on-line access to MEDLARS and POPLINE. Information queries received from users all over India are processed and information is disseminated through NICNET.

Small Enterprises National Documentation Centre (SENDOC). National Institute of Small Industry Extension and Training, Hyderabad

SENDOC was set up in 1971 to provide information support to technological and managerial advancement of small Industries. It offers various types of technical information services, prepares industry profiles and answers technical enquiries of a special nature. It has produced computerised product profiles (techno - economic information) besides index to product profiles.

UGC Information Centres (UGC-SIC) Smt. Nathibai Damodar Thackersey Women's University (SNDTWU) Bombay

The UGC established a Sectoral Information Centre at the SNDT women's University Library and Information Centre in 1986 for the subjects SOCIOLOGY, WOMEN'S STUDIES, HOME SCIENCE, SPECIAL EDUCATION, LIBRARY SCIENCE AND GUJARATI. Based on the information needs of researchers in these subject areas, the Centre decided to provide information services using primarily, a specially created database of Indian Research materials in ENGLISH, HINDI, GUJARATI and MARATHI languages. H.P. 3000/42 computer system and MINISIS software are used to create a database covering periodical articles since 1987 in the subject fields SOCIOLOGY, WOMEN'S STUDIES, and HOME SCIENCE. It is now extended to cover books and conference proceedings. Thesis and dissertations are included for early years as well. A union list of periodicals subscribed by various university, college and special libraries is maintained.

SYSTEMATIC APPROACH TO DATA SEARCH

The purpose is to provide some guides to the researcher to help in reviewing the literature; finding the sources of data; and the literature on subjects as exhaustive as possible. Following are some of the steps for the systematic approach in the documentary data search.

1. First, see your library catalogue under your subject area. You may note the subject headings listed at the bottom of each card. These subject heading will help you in knowing the subdivisions and related headings for further searching. See under more than one subject heading. This is the first checkpoint for your data-search.

2. Refer your subject area in the "Subject headings used in the Dictionary Catalogue of the library of Congress subject headings". It gives subject headings and cross references from all possible related headings.

3. Search your subject area in the various indexing services like "Business Periodical Index"; "Public Affairs Information Service"; and "Guide to Indian Periodical Literature", alongwith sub-divisions. The back volume of these services also may be referred. These are usually organized to provide information to source material.

4. Go through very carefully the subject bibliographies for possible source lists. You may refer the bibliographical collection of your as well as other outside libraries. Over and above, refer "Bibliographic Index": A cumulative Bibliography of Bibliographies 1937-; A Bibliography of Bibliographies in India - 1975; and A Bibliography of Indian Bibliographies: 1961-1980".

5. While going through the books and journals of your area, you will find the bibliographies given in the books at the end or at the chapter ends; and also the references and bibliographies cited at the end of the aritcles or in the footnotes of the articles. This is useful for a researcher

who need to build a literature review on a narrow topic in a limited time.

6. There are journals in which special sections on research studies/research in progress/theses completed etc. are regularly published. A list of such research included journals are listed under the heading 'Research Sources'. You may review such research issues of the various journals.

7. Look at the journals which are directly emenating from business schools and research institutes. A list of such journals is given.

8. You may also look for the research based articles on your subject.

9. Scan through various abstracts in the field like "Dissertation Abstracts" and the various listings of dissertations published as in the books or journals.

10. You may note down the library call nubmers of your subject area to browse in the stacks. Go through contents pages and bibliographies in potentially useful books.

11. As you go through the various references, you note down the bibliographics details of the references you think are useful for your subject on separate cards.

12. If possible, check with other specialist in the subject to determine if any major unsuspected source has been overlooked.

For all the methods of searching mentioned above, the researcher may proceed more rapidly if he or she has acquintance of using guides, abstracts, indexes, bibliographies and other sources.

EXHIBIT - I

SOME METHODICAL STEPS FOR RESEARCH/PROJECT WRITING

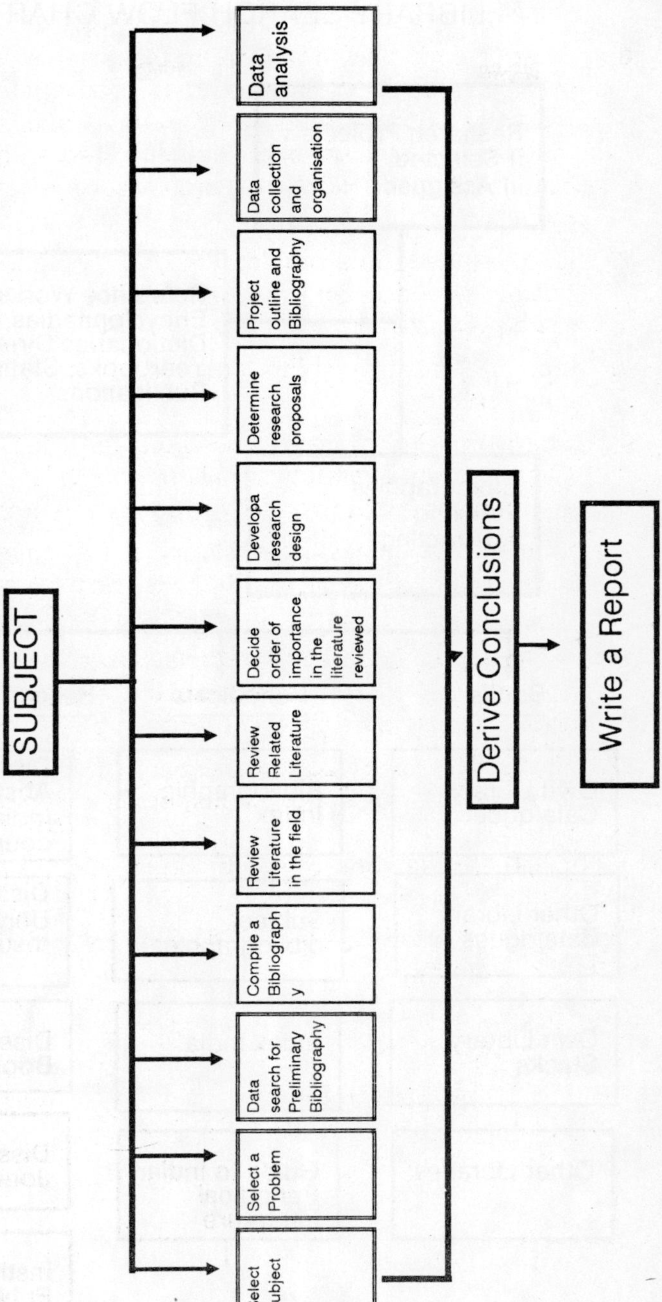

EXHIBIT - II
LIBRARY SEARCH FLOW CHART

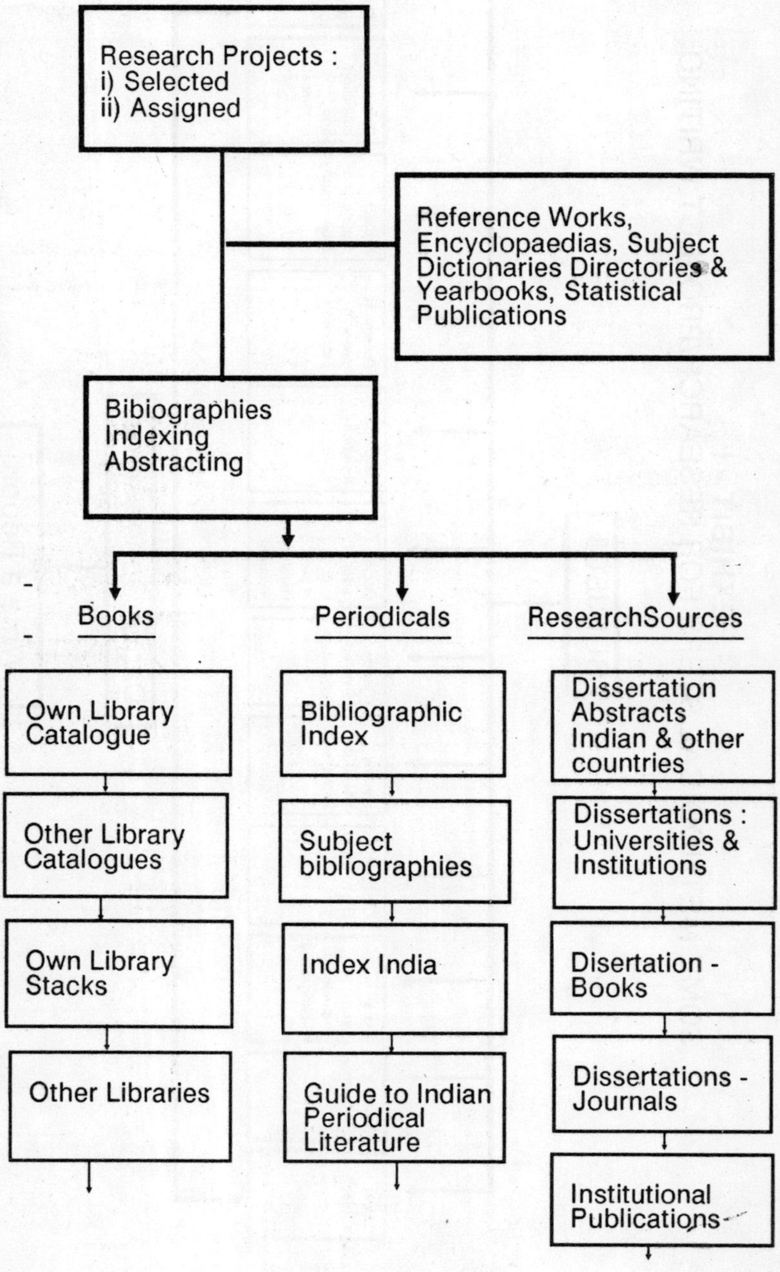

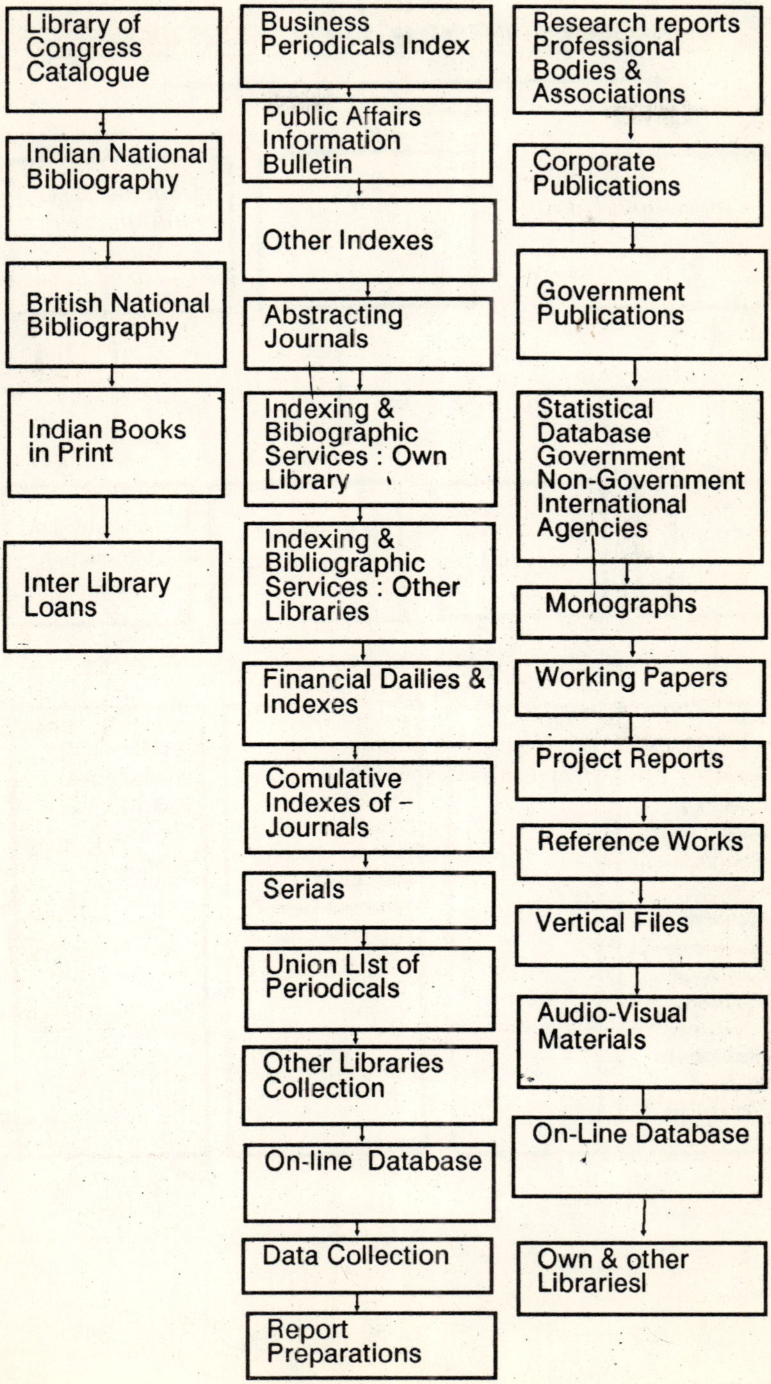
Library of Congress Catalogue
Indian National Bibliography
British National Bibliography
Indian Books in Print
Inter Library Loans
Business Periodicals Index
Public Affairs Information Bulletin
Other Indexes
Abstracting Journals
Indexing & Bibiographic Services : Own Library
Indexing & Bibliographic Services : Other Libraries
Financial Dailies & Indexes
Comulative Indexes of – Journals
Serials
Union LIst of Periodicals
Other Libraries Collection
On-line Database
Data Collection
Report Preparations
Research reports Professional Bodies & Associations
Corporate Publications
Government Publications
Statistical Database Government Non-Government International Agencies
Monographs
Working Papers
Project Reports
Reference Works
Vertical Files
Audio-Visual Materials
On-Line Database
Own & other Librariesl

EXHIBIT - III

MANAGEMENT INFORMATION SOURCES BY TYPES

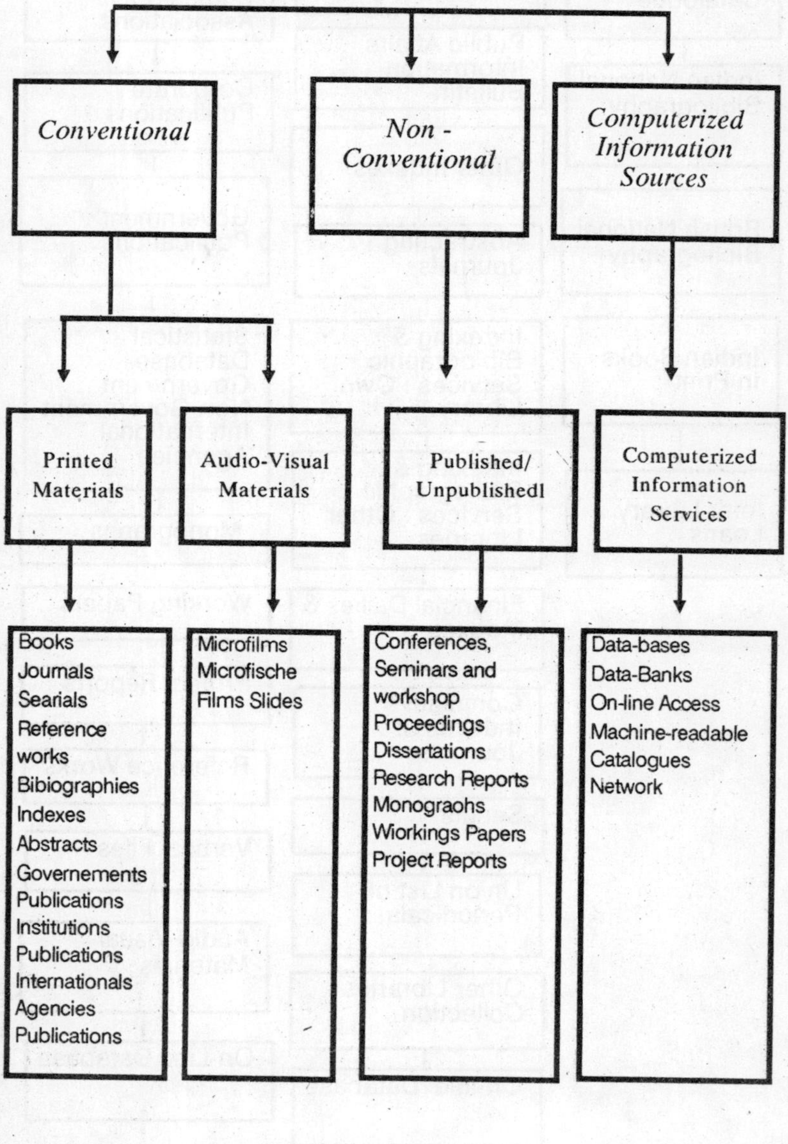

EXHIBIT - IV

MANAGEMENT INFORMATION SOURCES BY SUBJECTS

AGRICULTURE	COMPUTER AND INFORMATION SYSTEMS	ECONOMICS
Agricultural Policy	Systems Analysis & Simulation	Economic Analysis & Business Planning
Agricultural Management	Computer & System Software	Project Planning
Agricultural Finance	Decision Support Systems	International Trade
Forests & Forestry	Information Systems : Design & Implementation	International Banking & Finance
Food Sciences		Economic Enivronment & Policy
Co-operatives Management	Computer :	Games Theory & Applications
Agricultural Development Policies	Architecture & System Software	Business Forecasting
Agro-Industrial Projects		

FINANCE & ACCOUNTING	MANAGEMENT (BUSINESS POLICY)	MARKETING
Management Control System	Strategic Formulation & Implementation	Marketing Management
Investment & Poartfolio Management	Managerial oral Communication	International Marketing
International Finance	Corporate Planning	Product Policy & Mangement
Financial Institutions	International Business	Marketing Research & Information System
Corporate Finance	Public Enterprises Management	Industrial Marketing
Financial Management	Legal Aspects of Business	Advertising & Sales Promotion Management
Financial Accounting	Venture Management	Consumer movement
Cost Accounting	Strategic Management	Sales & Distribution Management
Financial System & Deveploment	Enterpreneurship	Logistics Management
	Corporate Tax Planning	

ORGANISATIONAL BEHAVIOR

- Human Resource Development
- Organizational Development
- Role and Identity
- Behavioral Sciences
- Creativity & Innovation
- Organizational Theory
- Institution Building
- Research methods
- Entrepreneurial Leadership
- Consulting Styles & Processes

PERSONNEL & INDUSTRIAL RELATIONS

- Strategic Human Resources
- Industrial Relations
- Personnel Management
- Training & Development
- Personnel Research

PRODUCTION & QUANTITATIVE METHODS

- Statistical Methods & Analysis
- Operations Research
- Quantitative Methods
- Manufacturing Policy & Innovations
- Materials Management
- Computer aided Decision Models
- Logistics & Physical Distribution System

PUBLIC SYSTEM

- Health & Population
- Public Management
- Urban Studies
- Development Administration
- Social Science & Policy
- Social Welfare & Development
- Economic Growth & Planning
- Education
- Energy
- Transportation
- Technological Innovations

APPENDIX - I
BIBLIOGRAPHY OF BOOKS ON RESEARCH METHODOLOGY

Abrahamson, Mark. SOCIAL RESEARCH METHODS. Englewood Cliffs, N.J., Prentice-Hall, 1983.

Alreck, P. and Settle, R. THE SURVEY RESEARCH HANDBOOK. Homewood, IL. Richard D. Irwin, 1985.

Berg, Bruce L. QUANTATIVE RESEARCH METHODS FOR THE SOCIAL SCIENCES. Boston, Allyn and Bacon, 1989.

Bhatnagar, O.P. RESEARCH METHODS AND MEASUREMENTS IN BEHAVIORAL SCIENCES. New Delhi, Agricole Pub., Academy, 1981.

Blalock, Hubert M. CONCEPTUALIZATION AND MEASUREMENT IN THE SOCIAL SCIENCE. Beverly Hills, Sage, 1982.

Black, James A. and Chaplon, D.J. METHODS AND ISSUES IN SOCIAL RESEARCH. New York, Wiley, 1976.

Blalock, H.M. and Blalock, A.B. METHODOLOGY IN SOCIAL RESEARCH. New York, Prentice-Hall, 1968.

Brinberg, David and McGrath, J.E. VALIDITY AND THE RESEARCH PROCESS. Beverly Hills, Sage Pub., 1985.

Bryman, Alan. RESEARCH METHODS AND ORGANIZATION STUDIES. London, Unwin Hyman, 1989.

Campbell, D.T. and Stanley, J.C. EXPERIMENTAL AND QUASI- EXPERIMENTAL DESIGNS FOR RESEARCH. Boston, Houghton Mifflin co., 1963.

Cavallo, Roger E. ROLE OF SYSTEMS METHODOLOGY IN SOCIAL SCIENCE RESEARCH. Boston, martinus Nijhoff, 1979.

Clover, V. and Balsey, H. BUSINESS RESEARCH METHODS. 2d ed. Columbus, Ohio, Grid, 1979.

Cooper, Harris. ON THE INTEGRATIVE RESEARCH REVIEW; A SYSTEMATIC APPROACH. Beverly Hills, Sage Publications, 1984.

Dasgupta, A.K. ed. METHODOLOGY OF ECONOMIC RESEARCH. Bombay, Asia, 1968.

Dasgupta, A.K. ed. RESEARCH METHODOLOGY IN ECONOMICS. Patna, Institute of World Studies.

Dasgupta, S. ed. METHODOLOGY OF SOCIAL SCIENCE RESEARCH. New Delhi, Impex India, 1967.

Desai, A.N. RESEARCH METHODOLOGY IN MANAGMENET. New Delhi, Ashish Pub. House, 1990.

Desai, H. G. and Desai, K.G. RESEARCH METHODS AND TECHNIQUES,2d ed. Ahmedabad, University BKS Production Board, 1979.

DEVELOPMENTS IN THE METHODOLOGY OF SOCIAL SCIENCE, ed. by Werner Leinfellner and Eckehart Kohler. Dordrecht etc. D. Reidel Pub. Co., 1974.

Dondyal, S.P. RESEARCH METHODOLOGY IN SOCIAL SCIENCES. Meerut, Friends' Publications, 1984.

Easterby-Smith, Mark and others. MANAGEMENT RESEARCH; AN INTRODUCTION. London, Sage Publications, 1991.

Emmert, P. and Brooks, W.D. eds. METHODS OF RESEARCH IN COMMUNICATION. Boston, Houghton-Mifflin, 1970.

Emory, C.W. BUSINESS RESEARCH METHODS. Homewood, IL. Richard D. Irwin, 1980.

Ferber, Robert and Verdoorn, P.J. RESEARCH METHODS IN ECONOMICS AND BUSINESS. New York, Macmillan, 1962.

Festinger, L. ed. RESEARCH METHODS IN THE BEHAVIOURAL SCIENCES. New York, Holt-Rinehart, 1953.

Forcesse, Dennis P. and Stephen Richer SOCIAL RESEARCH METHODS, Englewood Cliffs, N.J., Prentice-Hall, 1973.

Gee, Wilson. SOCIAL SCIENCE RESEARCH METHODS. New York, Appleton, 1950.

Ghosh, B.N. SCIENTIFIC METHOD AND SOCIAL RESEARCH. Delhi, India book House, 1983.

Hindess, Barry. PHILOSOPHY AND METHODOLOGY IN THE SOCIAL SCIENCES. Herssocks, Sussex, England: The Harvester Press, 1977.

Hirst, P. Q. SOCIAL EVOLUTION AND SOCIOLOGICAL CATEGORIES. London, Allen & Unwin, 1976.

Kaplan, Abraham. THE CONDUCT OF INQUIRY: METHODOLOGY FOR BEHAVIORAL/SCIENCE. San Francisco, Chandler, 1964.

Kaufmann, F. METHODOLOGY OF THE SOCIAL SCIENCES. New York, Humanities Press, 1958.

Kaul, L. METHODOLOGY OF EDUCATIONAL RESEARCH. New Delhi, Vikas, 1988.

Kerlinger, F.N. FOUNDATIONS OF BEHAVIORAL RESEARCH. 2d. ed. New York, Rinehart & Winston, 1973.

Kothari, C.R. RESEARCH METHODOLOGY: METHODS AND TECHNIQUES. New Delhi, Wiley Eastern, 1985.

Lazarsfeld, P. F. THE LANGUAGE OF SOCIAL RESEARCH: A READER IN THE METHODOLOGY OF SOCIAL RESEARCH, ed. by Paul F. Lazarsfeld and Morris Rosenberg. Glence, Ill., Free Press, 1955.

Lorie, J.H. and Roberts, H.V. BASIC METHODS OF MARKETING RESEARCH. McGrew-Hill, 1951.

McGrath, J.N. RESEARCH METHODS AND DESIGNS FOR EDUCATION. Scramton, Penn. International Textbook Co., 1970.

McGuigon, F. EXPERIMENTAL PSYCHOLOGY: A METHODOLOGICAL APPROACH. Englewood Cliffs, N.J. Prentice-Hall, 1978.

Machlup, Fritz. METHODOLOGY OF ECONOMICS AND OTHERS SOCIAL SCIENCES. New York, Academic Press, 1978.

Michael, V.P. RESEARCH METHODOLOGY IN MANAGEMENT, Bombay, Himalayan, 1985.

Misra, H.P. RESEARCH METHODOLOGICAL HANDBOOK. New Delhi, Concept, 1989.

Mohsin, S.M. RESEARCH METHODS IN BEHAVIOURAL SCIENCES. New Delhi, Orient Longman, 1984.

Nachmias, Chava and Nachmias, David. RESEARCH METHODS IN THE SOCIAL SCIENCES. London, Edward Arnold, 1981.

NEW TOOLS FOR SOCIAL SCIENTISTS; ADVANCES AND APPLICATIONS IN RESEARCH METHODS, ed. by W.D. Berry and M.S. Lewis-Beck, Beverly Hills, Sage Pub., 1986.

Norman, Richard. PERSONAL QUEST FOR METHODOLOGY. 3d. ed. Stockholm, SIAR Dokumentation, 1975.

O'Shaughnessy, John. INQUIRY AND DECISION: A METHODOLOGY FOR MANAGEMENT AND THE SOCIAL SCIENCES. New York, Barnes and Noble Books, 1973.

Patton, M. Q. QUANTITATIVE EVALUATION METHODS. Beverly Hills, Sage, 1980.

Prasad, D. RESEARCH METHODS IN SOCIAL SCIENCES. New Delhi, Sterling, 1989.

Price, J.L. and Mueller, C.W. HANDBOOK OF ORGANIZATIONAL MEASUREMENT. Marshfield MA: Pitman, 1986.

Rajammal, P. Devda and Kulandeivel, K. ed. 112 A HANDBOOK OF METHODOLOGY OF RESEARCH. Coimbatore, Sri Ramkrishna Mission Vidyalaya Teachers College, 1976.

Ramachandran, P. TRAINING IN RESEARCH METHODOLOGY IN SOCIAL SCIENCES IN INDIA. New Delhi, ICSSR, 1971.

Rande, A.C. RESEARCH METHODOLOGY IN SOCIAL SCIENCES. Delhi, Anmol Pub., 1989.

Reddy, C.R. RESEARCH METHODOLOGY IN SOCIAL SCIENCES. Delhi, Daya Pub. House, 1967.

RESEARCH METHODOLOGY IN SOCIAL SCIENCES IN INDIA, ed. by L.P. Vidyarthi and A.K. Haldaty. New Delhi, Today & Tomorrow's Printers and Publishers, 1985.

RESEARCH METHODS AND MEASUREMENTS IN BEHAVIOURAL AND SOCIAL SCIENCES. Delhi, Oxford and IBH., 1987.

RESEARCH RELATIONSHIP; PRACTICE AND POLITICS IN SOCIAL POLICY RESEARCH, ed. by G. Clare Wenger. London, Allen & Unwin, 1987.

Rosenthal, Robert and Rosnow, Ralph L. ESSENTIALS OF BEHAVIOURAL RESEARCH; METHODS AND DATA ANALYSIS. New York, McGraw-Hill, 1984.

Rummel, J.F. and Ballaine, W.S. RESEARCH METHODOLOGY IN BUSINESS. N.Y. Harper & Row, 1963.

Sadhu, A.N. and Singh, Amarjit. RESEARCH METHODOLOGY IN SOCIAL SCIENCES. Bombay, Himalaya Publishing House, 1983.

Selltiz, Claire and others. RESEARCH METHODS IN SOCIAL RELATIONS. New York, Holt, Rinehart and Winston, 1976.

Seminar on Research Methodology. RESEARCH METHODOLOGY; A SYMPOSIUM. Vallabha Vidhyanagar, Sardar Patel University, 1989.

Sethna, B.N. and Groeneveld, L. RESEARCH METHODS IN MARKETING AND MANAGEMENT. New Delhi, Tata McGraw-Hill, 1984.

Sharma, A.D. RESEARCH METHODS IN SOCIAL SCIENCES. New Delhi, NBO, 1988.

Shonts, F.C. RESEARCH METHODS IN PERSONALITY. New York, Appleton-Century-Crofts, 1965.

Sidhu, K.S. METHODOLOGY OF RESEARCH IN EDUCATION. New Delhi, Sterling Pub. Pvt. Ltd., 1984.

Simon, Julian Lincoln. BASIC RESEARCH METHODS IN SOCIAL SCIENCE; THE ART OF EMPIRICAL INVESTIGATION. New York, Random House, 1969.

Singh, Sadhu. RESEARCH METHODOLOGY IN SOCIAL SCIENCE. bombay, Himalaya, 1980.

Sjoberg, G. and Roger, N.D. A METHODOLOGY FOR SOCIAL RESEARCH. N.Y. Harper & Row, 1968.

Somachalam, K.S. RESEARCH METHODLOGY OF SOCIAL SCIENCES. Madurai, Kootder J. Publishers, 1978.

Srivastava, S.C. FORMULATIONS OF SOCIAL RESEARCH AND ECONOMETRIC TECHNIQUES. bombay, Himalaya, 1990.

Stone, Eugene. RESEARCH METHODS IN ORGANIZATIONAL BEHAVIOR. Santa Monica, Cal., Goodyear Pub. co., 1978.

Sutherland, John W. SOCIAL SYSTEM: METHODOLOGY MODELING AND MANAGEMENT. New York, North-Holland, 1978.

Tandon, B.C. RESEARCH METHODOLOGY IN SOCIAL SCIENCES. Allahabad, Chaitanya, 1979.

Verma, K. and Verma, Gopal. RESEARCH METHODOLOGY. New Delhi, Commonwealth, 1989.

Verma, S.L. RESEARCH METHODOLOGY IN POLITICAL SCIENCE: THEORY AND ANALYSIS. Jaipur, Rawat, 1989.

Waliser,M.H. and Wienir, P.L. RESEARCH METHODS AND ANALYSIS; SEARCHING FOR RELATIONSHIP. New York, Harper and Row, 1978.

Weber, Max. MAX WEBER ON THE METHODOLOGY OF THE SOCIAL SCIENCE, tr. and ed. by Edward A. Shils and Henry A. Finch. Glencoe, Ill., Free Press, 1949.

Wilkinson, T.S. and Bhandarkar, P.L. METHODOLOGY AND TECHNIQUES OF SOCIAL RESEARCH. Bombay, Himalaya Pub. House, 1982.

Yin, R.K. CASE STUDY RESEARCH, DESIGN AND METHODS. Beverly Hills, Sage Publications, 1984.

APPENDIX - II

BIBLIOGRAPHY OF BOOKS ON STYLE MANUALS & THESIS WRITING

Albough, Ralph N. THESES WRITING; A GUIDE TO SCHOLARLY STYLE, 1962.

American Institute of Physics. STYLE MANUAL. 3d. ed. New York, 1978.

American Psychological Association. PUBLICATION MANUAL. 2d ed. Washington, 1974.

Anderson, Jonathan. THESES AND ASSIGNMENT WRITING. New Delhi, Wiley Eastern Ltd., 1971.

Anthony Joseph, Alexis METHODOLOGY FOR RESEARCH GUIDE FOR WRITING DISSERTATIONS, THESES AND SCIENTIFIC PAPERS. Bangalore, Theological pub. in India, 1986.

Berenson, C, and Culton, R. RESEARCH AND REPORT WRITING FOR BUSINESS AND ECONOMICS. New York, Random House, 1971.

Billett, R.O. PREPARING THESES AND OTHER MANUSCRIPTS. New Delhi, Wiley, 1970.

Booth, V. WRITING A SCIENTIFIC PAPER. 4th ed. rev. Colchester Essex, Biochemical Society Book Depot, 1978.

Campbell, W.G. FORM AND STYLE IN THESIS WRITING. Massachusetts, Cambridge, 1958.

Chandra, Arvinda and Saxena, T.P. STYLE MANUAL FOR WRITING THESES, DISSERTATIONS AND PAPERS IN THE SOCIAL SCIENCES. New Delhi, Metropolitan book, 1979.

CHICAGO MANUAL OF STYLE: FOR AUTHORS, EDITORS AND COPYWRITERS. 13th ed. rev. and expanded. Chicago, University Press, 1982.

Cole, A.H. and Bigelow, K.W. A MANUAL OF THESES WRITING FOR GRADUATES AND UNDERGRADUATES. New York, John Wiley & Sons, 1956.

Council of Biology Editors (CBE). CBE STYLE MANUAL. 4th ed. Arlington, Va:, American Institute of Biological Sciences, 1978.

Davidson, D.E. THESES AND DISSERTATIONS AS INFORMATION SERVICES. London, c. Binglay, 1977.

Davis, G.B. and Donald, J.D. Mulkerene. WRITING FOR DOCTORAL DISSERTATIONS. Woodburg, N.Y., Barron's Educational Series, 1979.

EONOMIST POCKET STYLE BOOK. London, The Economist Publications, 1986.

Fletcher, J.A. and Gawing, D.F. BUSINESS GUIDE TO EFFECTIVE WRITING. London, Kogan Page, 1987.

Harman, E. and Montagnes, Ian eds. THE THESIS AND THE BOOK. New Delhi, Vistaar Publications, 1987.

Janis, J. Harold. THE BUSINESS RESEARCH PAPER; A MANUAL OF STYLE INCLUDING BIBLIOGRAPHICAL SOURCES FOR REPORTS, THESES, DISSERTATIONS. NY. Hobbs, Dorman & Co., 1967.

Koefod, Paul Eric. THE WRITING REQUIREMENTS FOR GRADUATE DEGREES. Englewood Cliffs, N.J., Prentice-Hall, 1964.

Manhermer, Martha L. STYLE MANUAL; A GUIDE FOR THE PREPARATION OF REPORTS AND DISSERTATIONS. New York, marcel Dekker, 1973.

Mitchell, J. HOW TO WRITE REPORTS. London, Fontana, 1978.

Modern Humanities Research Association. MHRA STYLE BOOK: NOTES FOR AUTHORS, EDITORS AND WRITERS OF DISSERTATIONS. 3d ed. London, 1986.

Modern Language Association of America. HANDBOOK FOR WRITERS OF RESEARCH PAPERS, by J. Giebaldi and W.S. Achtert. 2d ed. New Delhi, Wiley, 1984.

Mort, S. HOW TO WRITE SUCCESSFUL REPORT. London, Business Books, 1984.

Rao, S. Srinivas. HANDBOOK FOR WRITERS AND EDITORS. 3d rev. ed. Ahmedabad, Academic Book Centre, 1986.

Smith, Charles b. A GUIDE TO BUSINESS RESEARCH: DEVELOPING, CONDUCTING AND WRITING RESEARCH PROJECTS. Chicago, Nelson- Hall, 1981.

Sree, Ramulu, V.S. THESIS WRITING; BASIC PRINCIPLES. New Delhi, Oxford & IBH, 1988.

Strunk, W. jt. and White, E.G. THE ELEMENTS OF STYLE. 3d ed. London, collier Macmillan co., 1982.

Pugh, G. T. GUIDE TO RESEARCH WRITING. Boston, Houghton Mifflin.

Stuart, A. Richi ed. METHODS IN SOCIAL SCIENCES. Chicago, University of Chicago Press, 1981.

Syssams, J. E. HOW TO WRITE EFFECTIVE REPORTS. Aldershot, Hants, Gower, 1983.

Teitelbaum, Harry. HOW TO WRITE THESES; A GUIDE TO THE RESEARCH PAPER. New York, Monoveh Press, 1966.

Trelease, S. F. HOW TO WRITE SCIENTIFIC AND TECHNICAL PAPERS. Cambridge, Mass., MIT Press, 1969.

Turabian, Kate L. A MANUAL FOR WRITERS OF TERM PAPERS; THESES AND DISSERTATIONS. London, Heinemann, 1982.

APPENDIX - III
SOURCES CONSULTED

BOOKS

Agrawal, S.P. DEVELOPMENT OF LIBRARY SERVICES IN INDIA; SOCIAL SCIENCE INFORMATION. New Delhi, Concept, 1989.

Anderson, Dorothy. GUIDE TO INFORMATION SOURCES FOR THE PREPARATION, EDITING AND PRODUCTION OF DOCUMENTS. Aldershot, Gower, 1989.

Auger, Charles P. ed. USE OF REPORTS LITERATURE. London, Butterworths, 1975.

Backwell, K.G.B. BUSINESS INFORMATION AND THE PUBLIC LIBRARY. Brookfield, Gower, 1987.

Bakewell, K.G.B. HOW TO FIND OUT: MANAGEMENT AND PRODUCTIVITY, A GUIDE TO SOURCES OF INFORMATION ARRANGED ACCORDING TO THE UNIVERSAL DECIMAL CLASSIFICATION. 2d ed. Oxford, Pergamon, 1970.

Brophy, Peter. MANAGEMENT INFORMATION AND DECISION SUPPORT SYSTEMS IN LIBRARIES. Aldershot, Gower, 1986.

Compbell, Malcolm J. ed. MANUAL OF BUSINESS LIBRARY PRACTICE. London, Clive Bingley, 1975.

Dhekney, M.R. CHAMBERS OF COMMERCE AND BUSINESS ASSOCIATION IN INDIA. Bombay, Popular, 1971.

Easterby-Smith, Mark and others. MANAGEMENT RESEARCH; AN INTRODUCTION. London, Sage, 1991.

Emory, C. William. BUSINESS RESEARCH METHODS. Homewood, Irwin, 1976.

HANDBOOK OF LIBRARIES, ARCHIVES & INFORMATION CENTRES IN INDIA. ed. by B.M. Gupta and others. Information Industry Pub., 1984-85 -.

Huq, A.M. Abdul. GLOBAL ECONOMY; AN INFORMATION SOURCES.......... Phoenix, N.Y., Oryx Press, 1988.

India. Central Statistical Organisation. GUIDE TO OFFICIAL STATISTICS. 3d ed. New Delhi, C.S.O., 1987.

Johnson, H. Webster. HOW TO USE THE BUSINESS LIBRARY; WITH SOURCES OF BUSINESS INFORMATION. 4th ed. Cincinnati, South- Western Pub., 1972.

Kolatkar, Ram S. FINDING THE FACTS; NEWSPAPER, INFORMATION RETRIEVAL SYSTEM. New Delhi, Press Institute of India, n.d.

Kurien, C.T. ed. GUIDE TO RESEARCH IN ECONOMICS. 2nd Ed. Coimbatore, Rainbow, 1985/

Lal, Chhotey, and Ahsan, A. Shoaib. A GUIDE TO REFERENCE SOURCES IN AGRICULTURE AND BIOLOGICAL SCIENCES. Delhi, Bharati Publications, 1989.

Maltby, Arthur. ECONOMICS AND COMMERCE; THE SOURCES OF INFORMATION AND THEIR ORGANISATION. Hamden, Connecticut, Archon Books, 1968.

Meltzer, Morton F. INFORMATION CENTER; MANAGEMENT HIDDEN ASSET. New York, American Management Association, 1967.

Murdick, Robert G. and Cooper, D.R. BUSINESS RESEARCH; CONCEPTS AND GUIDES. Columbus, Grid Publishing, 1982.

Pandya, J.F. and others. INFORMATION SOURCES FOR BUSINESS AND INDUSTRY. Ahmedabad, B.S. Shah Prakashan, 1980.

Parker, C.C. and Turley, R.V. INFORMATION SOURCES IN SCIENCE AND TECHNOLOGY. London, butterworths, 1976.

Parsons, S.A.J. HOW TO FIND OUT ABOUT ECONOMICS. Oxford, Pergamon Press, 1972.

Schlessinger, Bernard S. BASIC BUSINESS LIBRARY: CORE RESOURCES. Phoenix, Oryx Press, 1983.

Sharma, H.D. and Mukherji, S.P. RESEARCH IN ECONOMICS AND COMMERCE, METHODOLOGY AND SOURCES. Varanasi, Indian bibliographic Centre, 1976.

Smith, charles B. A GUIDE TO BUSINESS RESEARCH: DEVELOPING, CONDUCTING AND WRITING RESEARCH PROJECTS. Chicago, Nelson- Hall, 1981.

Stewart, David W. SECONDARY RESEARCH; INFORMATION SOURCES AND METHODS. London, Sage, 1984.

Tega, Vasile G. MANAGEMENT AND ECONOMCIS JOURNALS; A GUIDE TO INFORMATION SOURCES. Detroit, Gale Research Company, 1977.

Vernon, Ken ed. LIBRARY AND INFORMATION SERVICES OF MANAGEMENT DEVELOPMENT INSTITUTIONS; A PRACTICAL GUIDE. Geneva, ILO, 1986.

Verman, K.D.C. ed. INFORMATION SOURCERS IN MANAGEMENT AND BUSINESS. 2d ed. London, butterworths, 1984.

ARTICLES

Coe, Robert and Weinstock, Irwin. Evaluating the management journals: a second look. ACADEMY OF MANAGEMENT JOURNAL, vol. 27, no. 3, 1984. 660-666.

Sharplin, Arthur D. and Mabry, Rodney, H. Relative importance of Journals used in management research: an alternative ranking. HUMAN RELATIONS, vol. 38, no. 2, 1985. 139-149.

Stahl, Michael J. and others. Publication in leading management journals as a measure of institutional research productivity. ACADEMY OF MANAGEMENT JOURNAL, vol. 31, no. 3, 1988. 707- 720.